Old Harry's Bunkside Book

A collection of the 'Old Harry' stories originally published in Yachts and Yachting *and* Yachting Monthly.

Written and illustrated by J.D. Sleightholme.

ADLARD COLES LIMITED
GRANADA PUBLISHING
London Toronto Sydney New York

by the same author
Cruising: A Manual for the Small Sailing Boat Owner
Fitting Out: Maintenance and Repair of Small Craft
ABC for Yachtsmen

Published by Granada Publishing in
Adlard Coles Limited, 1978

Granada Publishing Limited
Frogmore, St Albans, Herts AL2 2NF
and
3 Upper James Street, London W1R 4BP
1221 Avenue of the Americas, New York, NY 10020 USA
117 York Street, Sydney, NSW 2000, Australia
100 Skyway Avenue, Toronto, Ontario, Canada M9W 3A6
Trio City, Coventry Street, Johannesburg 2001, South Africa
CML Centre, Queen and Wyndham, Auckland 1, New Zealand

Copyright © J.D. Sleightholme, 1978

Printed in the United States of America

All rights reserved. No part of this publication may be reproduced,
stored in a retrieval system, or transmitted, in any form or by any means,
electronic, mechanical, photocopying, recording or otherwise, without
the prior permission of the publisher.

Contents

INTRODUCTION   5
THE SOCIAL SCENE
    Try some of mine   6
    Lend us a hand   8
    Rally round the flag   9
    At home   11
    Mould me a character   13
    A first rate chep   15
    Make yourself at home   17

FITTING OUT AND LAYING UP
    Not a patch on it   19
    Let all the family help   21
    The finishing touch   23
    It's hardly fitting   25
    A show of hands   26
    You can't go wrong in the airing cupboard   28

DRESS
    Well turned out   31
    Knit one purl one   33
    I find it a dreadful tie   35

NAVIGATION
    A spell with the bottles   37
    It puts me in a funny position   39

SEAMANSHIP

Its all right once you're in	42
I heard a little hiss	44
Comic turn	46
Who said 'let go'?	48
Marina amenities	50
Don't just stand there	53

FINANCE AND FIGURES

Immaculate condition	56
Met trickery	58
A hard case	60
A flare for invention	61

Introduction

SINCE 1959, WHEN Old Harry first appeared on the scene, I seem to have written around one hundred and fifty short pieces about him. I was on the staff of *Yachts and Yachting* then and Old Harry was an accidental invention, based subconsciously upon just about every obdurate, bloody minded traditionalist of inventive turn that I had ever chanced to meet. The Old Harry drawing, invented at the same time, has by sour coincidence come home to roost nearly twenty years later; I am assured by those around me that I have grown to look exactly like him.

Prior to being taken over by my creation I had been inclined to sneer in fine contempt at writers who talked about giving 'life' to their characters. It smacked of a mimsy conceit, dirndl skirts and a mucky kitchen. The fact of the matter is that it is readers who force life into the monster, pull the switch and let loose the lightning and the author does damn-all. The Old Harry image now hangs around my neck with every mooring buoy I miss and with every sewer outfall pipe I hit.

Sailing and yacht clubs everywhere seem to claim at least one Old Harry among their membership – a claim inspired more by resignation than pride. I have picked around in a heap to select a representative collection, all of which have appeared in print either in *Yachts and Yachting* or in more recent years in *Yachting Monthly*. I am grateful to Peter Cooke, editor of the former and to my own publishers IPC Magazines Ltd for permission to present Old Harry in book form.

JDS

The Social Scene

I'M NOT EXACTLY antisocial, it's just that social occasions tend to take the pea out of my whistle. The first time I wore full evening dress I changed in the hotel gents, standing in the lid of Moss Bros' cardboard box. I got the tabs on the dicky hooked up to the wrong deadeyes and emerged bent double in a sort of courtly bow, only permanent. I daren't straighten up in case I shot someone with a button.

Cocktail parties I loathe. My voice lacks penetration at conversation level and neither can I hear above that racket; I end up squeaking like a hamster. Then there are dinner guests who won't go. You could have the Town Hall clock on the mantlepiece and they wouldn't notice it. 'Ah well' you hint, standing with the cat under your arm. They sit it out like NHS patients frightened to reveal their particulars.

Then there's youth training. I spent two years as an instructor with the Outward Bound Sea School breathing through my nose, thinking clean thoughts and taking cold showers; I ended up with flaring nostrils, a shifty eye and wrinkled like a prune. In shorts I looked like a couple of earwig traps. Crewing, harks back to my days on the RORC Crew List doing pierhead jumps. I got everything from the spearhead nobility with a crew of Aussies in bush hats and jock straps to Class Three draggle-tails where you raced like demons until ten minutes after the gun, then put Percy on the wheel and fell in astern of the fleet like a dustcart behind a carnival.

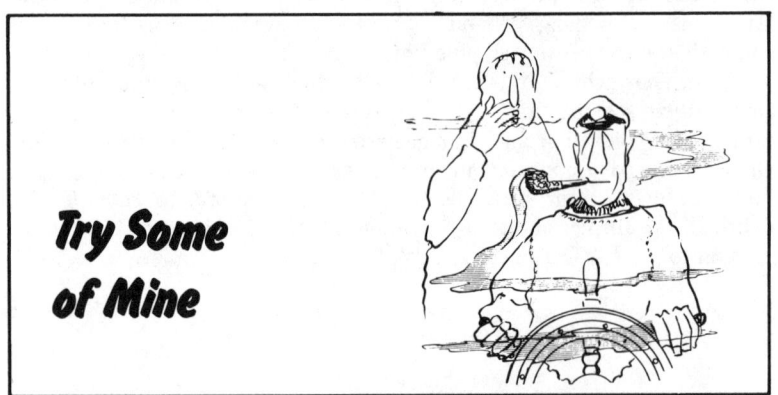

Try Some of Mine

THE GREAT TRADITION of square-jawed cruising yachtsmen seated at the wheel with rough briar clamped in strong white teeth dies hard on the modern offshore racer. What with the apparent wind fluting straight up his dottle-trap and the owner making fine dumb crambo of clawing ash out of his eyes our helmsman is left gingerly biting his stem between front teeth like a dog registering repugnance for an unwanted biscuit.

'Light a tube for the helmsman', other shipmates may confide in reverent tones.

'He's been on for three hours', they add, as if he was hatching an egg.

Watched by resentful eyes lest he take a hand off the spokes, he must derive what nourishment he can while it sizzles away like a sulphur candle in a rat hole.

Advertisements paint a misleading picture of the rollicking life afloat, they show a rugged yachtsman crinkling his eyes at the camera while he lets go a sigh of content that would blast the bobbin out of your Ventimeter — this is a *calm moment.* In practise it doesn't always work out. Calm moments are as rare as cricket caps at a May-Day rally.

'Here's a *"calm moment"* coming!' alerts the helmsman bobbing about ready to grab it.

All hands fumble feverishly with matches and get in one furtive drag before the owner thinks up a sail-change. We've seen Percy in the pulpit grabbing a calm moment behind the luff of the jib.

'How's your luff!' trumpets the mate of the watch, spotting him at it.

Percy struggles to his feet jetting smoke like a trick Buddha in nice time to stop a sea. The extinguished butt trembling on indignant lip unfolds slowly like a rare bud in a nature film. Old Harry with a 'baccy pouch like a sporran and a private cumulo-nimbus cloud overhead is something of an authority on the pipe. Americans with their little bags of dust win a ready sympathy from him.

'Here', he'll say, rocking with mirth at their attempts to smoke, 'you'll get some benefit from this!'

He proceeds to carve slices from a grisly fossil which has the consistency of a stopper knot. You'll see them whooping and gasping around the deck, gripping their throats and rolling up eyes like pickled eggs on a billiards table as they stammer their gratitude while the greenish fumes coil knee-deep.

There are times when his presence below deck wins him a dubious welcome from those whose eyes have taken on a certain fixity. While they whistle shakily to take their minds off the dreadful sight. Harry is digging away at the bowl of his pipe with a nail.

'Look at that lot!' he'll command thrusting it forward for closer inspection. Upper bunk inmates quit the sack like firemen rallying to the bell.

Since he discovered Impi Twist Harry has given up growing his own leaf. He once reared stout hedges of it which had to be harvested with an axe. Spread liberally with rum and molasses and seasoning on his coach roof it provided welcome fare for scavenging gannets. We have seen a fowl seize upon a leaf, pause and then rocket skywards only to plunge seawards in haste following a rolling Falstaffian burp.

Old Harry's visits to a foreign shore are seldom without incident. There was the occasion when he called at a fuel depot for a bucket of petrol. A sign which read *'Defense de Fumer'* caught his eye but taking it to be some form of political slogan he glanced decently aside in true British embarrassment at this emotional display.

'Alors, alors attention, monsieur!' cried a little man from the office. *'You are smock le pip!'*

Outraged at this frivolous case of mistaken identity and roaring his name for the simple fellow's benefit Harry strode forward belching smoke

Old Harry's Bunkside Book

and sparks like a riveter's bogy. Overcome by this stern show of authority the attendant was seen to go streaking up the road, sandals rattling like a supermarket till.

Harry's good opinion of the nation was not fully restored until the time came when he ran short of plug. Rapping the grocer's counter with a specimen and enunciating at full volume he commanded immediate attention.

'Poor lee pipe'o' he explained fluently.

The hunk of liver sausage yielded by this exchange he voted a stylish smoke although a bit fancy for his tastes.

THOSE MAGAZINE PICTURES which show club members clustered dubiously round a cement mixer in the thin December drizzle, like volunteer yeomanry off to the Crimea or staggering round in a hole trying to dislodge plugs of clay from their shovels are a direct indictment of all us Bad Club Members. The call for willing hands to improve club facilities wakes empty echoes in guilty ears.

'What a pity', we mourn, injecting drama-group tragedy into our voices, *'this* Saturday looks like being a tricky day for me!' No understatement this, it'll call for a light foot and a nimble turn of speed at street corners if we are to avoid meeting our Commodore pushing a barrow.

In Old Harry's case every effort is made to conceal from him signs of impending industry and the fine military bearing of club members converging on the job with shovels up their coveralls has aroused favourable comment.

Fancying his luck as a bricklayer he has raised a series of unsteady edifices on the club's behalf. Building by eye and scorning the use of plumb-bob and level his walls acquire the dignity of age before the mortar is dry. Antiquarians, new to the district ('Am I all right for the burial mound?') have been known to stand moist-eyed with respect for vanished glories until Old Harry, followed by his dog (which has a passable likeness to Judge Jefferies on all fours) comes in sight with loaded barrow thundering along a plank. I have seen a visiting Borough Surveyor in pork pie and gum boots, clutch his bye-laws and leap for sanctuary down a soak-pit, one hop ahead of this imminent peril, only to receive a load of coarse aggregate down the welcoming waistband of his Wolseys.

Old Harry's Bunkside Book

In no mood to be gracious about a drainage system which wanders creekwards like a thirsty traveller in search of an oasis and which Harry, with the alert and canny mistrust of a dog with a bone, has just buried, he orders it exhumed. With breath rasping harshly in his throat, knees bent and vibrating under this hellish strain, like a Highlander with his sporran in the mangle, Old Harry voices his displeasure in tones which reduce our fellow to forelock tugging apology.

The clubs which build new premises from scratch suffer a dispiriting blow to morale when they see the finished product. The architect's drawing, all tricked out in water-colours and miniature members, implies a UNO building in asbestos and beaverboard. Reality reveals it as a Spartan little go-down approached by a duckboard causeway that squirts water up your trouser-leg via a system of knot-holes. Inside decorations (knotty pine wallpaper and tea-urn on card table) show that ingenuity has been given full reign and the visitor, his gaze circulating walls, floor and ceiling like a Polyphoto sitter, murmurs his admiration.

'I like the way you've adapted old barrels as bar stools' he chuckles, crashing to earth.

Converters of old property win our deepest admiration.

'It all comes down to using your head a bit' they muse, slapping a wall with exploratory fist – a descending pancake of ceiling plaster instantly caps our thinker, lending him the brief dignity of a stone apostle on a church porch which points cautionary finger at its whitewashed dome.

It is the plasterer's ancient art which routs most enthusiasts. With easy assurance they slap one helping on the wall as if buttering a bun and have nice time in which to stoop for the next when the first lands with the dull thud of a school omelette on their necks. Old Harry on the other hand, using dustpan and fish-slice, keeps up a rapid bombardment which bodes ill for the curious bystander.

Rally Round the Flag

I HAVEN'T SEEN a really good rally since the time Old Harry dropped a sack of parrel beads down Holborn escalator at rush hour. In the high old days of pitchpine bowsprits a good cruiser rally was like attending a Mayoral reception with a ladder under your arm; if you didn't wake up with a cranse iron up your scrollwork you were either aground or dragging.

There is a nice difference between the club and the class rally. The aim

Old Harry's Bunkside Book

at club rallies is for the bigger boats to compete in seeing how many guests they can get aboard at one time.

'We had thirty at Whitsun' brags the owner of a converted harbour launch with a potting shed built on it.

They were plastered all over it like winter migrants, clutching empty paper cups and shuddering in the bleak wind of twilight.

Your class rally (presided over by the builder, heavily benign like a Police Inspector giving a school lecture) radiates a sense of unity varying in degree according to how bad the boat happens to be to windward. Local Dragon owners sneering thinly, tack through the anchorage gazing straight ahead with narrowed eyes as if nervous of being asked to judge a cake. The class rally also offers an opportunity to examine the other man's boat for ideas.

'Look where he's put his little tell-tale then', comments an owner gazing admiringly through someone else's porthole.

There is a scuffle from within and a curtain is drawn. Later in the year there will be a dinner and film show which, damned by faulty exposure, shows pale figures, corpse-like of complexion, leaping around untypically against a yellow sea. The wag of the party with waxen grin toasts the camera with pink beer.

The arrival of Old Harry, who loves a rally whether invited or not, is noted by the organiser with a numbing sense of prophecy. No witch doctor, divining sheep's entrails and coming across a cracker joke, motto and cap, is more gloomily concerned for the portents than this unhappy man as he watches the approaching bowsprit. In clean cardboard collar and festive mood Old Harry notes the stir of activity with pleasure.

'Let's see if we can enter into things with a bit 'o style.' he chuckles.

Carrying more headway than a cloakroom attendant sighting fluff his bowsprit enters into things via the open companionway of a small plastics cruiser; it emerges dripping with custard.

Early mornings impose a severe strain on the collective diplomacy of rallyists. Pyjama clad husbands emerge from their cabins champing their gums, searching for the milk and turning on gas bottles.

'Thaff the laff time I truff you to gueff the gaff preffure,' comments a spouse bitterly, his taut Paisley rump adding a needed touch of heraldry.

The important thing is a mutual and unspoken agreement to keep gazes lowered, thus eyes do not meet and civilities do not therefore have to be exchanged. Elsewhere, in the smaller boats, a scattering of husbands all gaily caparisoned like a circus act stand around in their cockpits pretending to take a morning breath of fresh air in a biting salty blast that would take the buttons off a hospital sofa. The boats heave and jerk to the convulsions of wives completing an acrobatic toilet below.

The preparation of the main evening meal can become bitterly competitive. The cruising family accustomed to the evening basic of beans and bangers, with fruit, cheese or lump it to follow turn reproachful eyes on mother as taunting aromas waft over from the craft alongside. There is a 10 year old girl whose sole duty is to report on what other people are cooking.

'We're having raspberry flan and cream,' she crows gazing like a laser beam at the individual fruit soggies in their individual cardboard boxes. Her gaze down an open forehatch can rout its occupants like a blast of creosote up a hollow log.

Much as Old Harry enjoys a rally he guards the solitude of his favourite creek jealously. Let him but find it tenanted by one small boat and its white knee'd owner in school knickers and he is beside himself.

'Look' he roars, 'the place is *solid* with 'em.'

He anchors half a mile away and settles down with the binoculars to study every movement made by the enemy, maintaining a scornful commentary on boat, seamanship and personal habits.

The search for solitude affects many of us. Your anti-rallyist seeks out haunts of coot and tern with the avidity of lovers looking for long grass. You find him, at low water, at the top end of a creek where he floats in a trickle like a beef olive in a pool of gravy. Wives suffer these trysts with nature in cynical silence. Plodding ashore ('There's a useful little hard over there dear') and knee deep in it with shopping bag, milk tin, water carrier, purse, headscarf and oily jacket – it turns blazing hot 10 minutes later – she tackles a succession of five-barred gates, pursued by fascinated cattle and has to explain things to a farmer. She arrives at the village and finds the shop shut. Father, who has been 'getting a few jobs done on board,' a task calling for tinned ale and sunawning, notes the silent and non-waving figure on the beach with the sinking spirits of a theatre patient studying his painted abdomen.

At Home

A glittering scene and the ball of wit tossed lightly to and fro.

I'VE BEEN TO some At Homes in my time. They vary from select gather-trying to grip a sherry glass without showing your fingernails, to all-in shindies where you are lucky to get away with your trousers.

The At Home offers the boldest challenge of all social occasions to both host and guest but for club hosts there is the added necessity to keep everybody topped up and talking. Club wives are on their mettle at this game. We see a wife draped in crochet-work and of vast fore and aft development so that she looks like a medieval hobbyhorse, dispatching her husband to flush lone visitors away from their unseeing perusal of the

Old Harry's Bunkside Book

notice-board. 'Keep circulating dear,' she hisses, as if he were some sort of hot water system. 'Go and TALK to them.'

There is an art to this. Once you can get a group of guests together you call over another circulating host for introductions. You then back slowly away, smiling freely and nodding, leaving your group nucleated around your unwilling replacement in a similar manner to that employed by the wily fox which rids itself of fleas by backing slowly, muzzle-deep into river or pool.

There will be the guests who are unashamedly out for a skinful and those who are 'just going to show their faces for a few minutes' – a treat which implies sudden appearance at a window and a quick intake of breath from the assembly inside. Either way the idea of the game is to prevent them from buying their own drinks. The first arrivals (who have been sitting it out in their cars for the last half-hour, intent upon avoiding this very situation) wander into the clubhouse with the wary compulsion of ducks entering a decoy pond, electing not to hear the cries of urgent alarm from within. They stand dodging around each other just inside the door, trying out all their pockets with different hands, unwilling to make for the bar. An unwilling host member (who had only come to read the notice-board) finds himself lumbered. 'You'd better have a drink,' he states, lugging his wallet out and trying to inject a note of hospitality into his tone. He sounds more like an out-patients' sister offering regulation succour to a recovering poultice case.

The guests too must note certain rules. If they are to be plied with refreshment like nestlings they must regulate their rate of intake to the munificence of their immediate hosts who may either watch the level in the glasses as if reading a steam gauge or ('well, that's my lot!') leave their guests to sip at the last half-inch with the tardiness of worker-bees probing a joke button-hole. There is the further complication of carrying fresh supplies across a crowded floor.

The normal tactic is to back, rump first, into the press unmindful of the peppering of ash, crumb and spillage collected on the butt end; the more courtly frontal attack calls for some delicacy in passing astern of the ladies rather than risk some canon of plunging necklines. Old Harry, with three pints in each hand, held high and fingers fully immersed, shows no hesitation on such occasions. There was the time when the inevitable happened. Placing his precious cargo on a handy chair he at once rendered assistance to the lady who, hysterically refusing his practical solution of a wadded newspaper which he attempted to lodge in position to serve as an absorbent dicky, swooned prettily into the chair. Which was a pity.

Old Harry, who could make himself at home at a diocesan conference, never misses these functions. Arriving first and leaving under power (with a hand under each elbow) last, he leads his trotting host to the bar, pausing only to scan new applications for club membership on the board and to offer confidential albeit laughing comment on their chances. A club matron, bending to her artistic work with the parsley, springs erect with a whoop of disapproval. Doffing his cap to the ladies, while mindful of the tobacco pouch therein, he passes among the men dealing many a comrade-

Old Harry's Bunkside Book

ly slap on the back. They lift dripping muzzles from their pints and gaze without warmth at his wake.

The evening winds to its close. The last sausage rolls, rattling like a witch-doctor's gourd, are collected by their donors for extended service in lunch-boxes throughout the week and the commodore has made his short, good humoured and totally inaudible speech of welcome; stern cries of QUIET! brought a sudden silence in which he was left piping like a boy soprano. Guests who had anticipated an evening of gay verbal exchange have been stuck with founder members of interminable reminiscence, wobbling chin and empty glass. There remains The-Man-who-won't-be-invited-next-time. With a lock of hair over one eye he is singing from one side of his mouth through lips extensile as a dentist's bib. He makes his stiff-legged, tuneless way from shoulder to shoulder and is last seen hunting up and down in the hedge in search of a gate.

TO REALISE THAT the sea is a powerful character-moulder we have only to take Old Harry (preferably in a fall-trap!). Forty-years of wet bunks and dry biscuits has twisted his psyche like a trombone. The average yachtsman with his swivelling eye and shambling half-trot makes the point clear enough to say nothing of those poor, mad creatures in tattered P.V.C. who haunt marsh and sedge armed with a winch handle and hunting the Water Rat.

Every man cherishes a memory of himself as a lad – not the image in velveteen and Jackie Coogan cap stuffing calves-foot jelly and standing on the chemist's scales, but a stocky little chap with gurgling laugh and open visage (like a Continental plumbing system) walking five miles to school through a perpetual snowstorm. Lacking similar amenities for his own lad he turns to sea and cocoa in equal proportions. There is something about the good life of wind and canvas – the healthy challenge of it, the laughing comradeship.

Take for instance picking up the mooring, a typical family exercise loaded with spiritual nourishment. With the lad on the foredeck bobbing his great flat head in the way and dad on the stick yelling 'Tell me when I'm on' and nipping from seat to side-deck and back like a wild bird in a cage, a great sense of manly one-ness is born. With howls of 'Have you got it, boy?' he takes her past the buoy at a thunderous pace only to do his

Old Harry's Bunkside Book

Macbeth-and-the-dagger act as his stupified eye follows the buoy in its flight past.

As the evolutions gain in originality and decrease in diameter, Mother's head appears in the forehatch ('That's no way to address your father') and then reappears aft ('Not THAT word if you please'). The mating flight of the snipe is a laughable amateur frolic compared to a bit of character-moulding in full swing. On the club verandah watchers wince and cover their eyes, reluctant to note the inevitable outcome of an ever-decreasing circle.

Not all our lads seem to realize what we are trying to do for them. Lads with regulation forelock and wise old eyes, one ear permanently bleached and flattened by the transistor, watch curiously as we thunder round our decks drawing deep, whistling breaths and glaring fiercely at the horizon.

'This'll make men of you' we pipe shrilly, cutting off their supply of beer and baccy and urging them under the cold showers as if they had caught fire. Six foot of codliver oil and rosehip syrup frowns down at us with menace.

Some of the youngsters (pronounced yangsters) take to it at once. In one season they are qualified to line the banks, eyes dimmed with uncontrollable mirth as they watch their elders creaking around the windward mark. Huge cadets, haunched like prime baconers with five o'clock shadow, crouch in diminutive dinghies and wait to be fed with trophies while harassed family men (paid up members) who can only fan the air with folding money between p.m. Friday and a.m. Saturday chalk up another five bob on yet another Junior cadet fund list. It's worth any sacrifice though.

'I can see the change in my lad' grunts a father, twitching. His eyes are bright with pride as he watches some hollow-bowed youth with shoulderblades like a test-your-grip machine running a club boat up the ramp with a judder.

Nowadays anyone owning forty-feet of wet oak and fungus with ratlines and a pitch-pine proboscis is automatically marked down as a training man. Six lads and a bugle and you have every well-wisher in a twelve mile radius pelting you with medicine balls and rough blankets. Men in executive greatcoats and fine leonine profiles hasten to congratulate you on doing a Fine Job.

Old Harry whose ship meets practically every requirement and who hoped to qualify for school milk on the strength of his break-back windlass once netted ten copies of 'Black Beauty' and a gross of bean bags — it did, however, arouse his interest in youth training. Born in an era when bucko mates could mould you a character in the brief time it took to crawl from doss-house to main futtocks, his theories, if sound, met with little popular support and an early attempt to enter for the Sail Training Race was frustrated when his stores were checked — two sacks of split peas, and three of holystones.

There is a sad belief that in order to do any good for the lads one must first attempt to look like one. The full-time instructor clad in duffle and

Old Harry's Bunkside Book

fur mitts for the morning dip lacks the keen edge of enthusiasm shown by down-for-the-day high-ranking Min. of Ed. officials. They appear on deck, bare knees like a set of jugs, and take up their stand on the mainsheet glaring around like herons alert for the gyrfalcon. They take miles of ciné film of lads shading their eyes and depart on the five-thirty full of cocoa and fresh air.

Lads like a sense of purpose. Hot from his drum set our son may have to be persuaded that a rainy night off the Nore going nowhere and for no particular reason is in some way beneficial. Harry's solution to lack of purpose is to pay them in advance, take it off them with the pea and thimble trick and keep them working off the dead horse for the following fortnight. His one excursion into this field saw rich dividends, a return from foreign parts heralded by the Diplomatic Bag and preceded by a flight of searching helicopters.

A First Rate Chep

THE 'OWNER SEEKS Crew' and 'Crew Seeks Berth' announcements in the small ad columns hint at some shadowy game of hide-and-seek wherein owners poke with sticks under old boats and crews try out berth after berth sighing fastidiously at the quality of flock and springing (at that it is not unknown for an owner to tiptoe silently through his sleeping heap in search of any rude pallet where he might lay his head).

The ideal crew is a man of tact. He realizes that on the family cruiser the hand-bearing compass is the owner's symbol of authority — a maritime mace which stands for the lonely pinnacle of responsibility and skipperdom. The hand who will make play lightly with this instrument can expect to see some ginger, by heaven!

'All right, I'll take that," whips out our owner, grabbing his dolly.

He claps it to his eye and peers around, mumbling like some witchdoctor smelling out devils.

Nowadays the crew's union is all-powerful. Not for nothing was that ghastly term 'crew-member' substituted for plain old-fashioned 'hand'. An owner must be lovable if he is going to keep his little band.

'My old owner never raised his voice save in laughter,' says a hand as he sobs hysterically at a missed mooring.

For the new hand, more to be feared than an owner's displeasure, are the regulars who have crewed for him for at least two years running. The

Old Harry's Bunkside Book

new hand, desperate to please, starts by tearing around giving a shrill and solitary laugh whenever he lays hand to the wrong rope. His babbled tales of derring-do on previous ships fall on deaf ears. Not until he has damned himself by crossing his turns or turned in with the owner's foam-filled pillow is he allowed to walk on his hind legs as a fellow-man.

The other side of the coin spells disaster to our regular residents. The owner discovers a miracle-man oddly overlooked by other owners.

'This is Lieut. Commander Snarp,' he introduces carefully.

'Just call me Teony,' laughs this mariner from somewhere in the deep shadows beneath his peak.

The carefree days of gross inefficiency are at an end. 'If I may make a little suggestion,' becomes the opening remark to a stark new order. This paragon, henceforth never to be seen fully out of the main hatchway, bombards owner and crew with little suggestions accompanied by piercing cries of 'Check, check, check,' like some startled wildfowl at eventide. The owner slinks below to brood over his cheque book stubs and leaves it to his crew to work out a happy compromise based on a smart luff and a breaking sea.

Club get-togethers and crew questionnaires provide a sort of mop fair for the introduction of the pipe-cot jockeys to the crewless. Owners strive for a mien of benign and steadfast purpose while prospective crews, by means of unlimited reminiscing, outline their talents. We could develop the idea. Navigators might sidle around shyly exhibiting charts covered with tiny cocked hats and foredeck hands could lope around the room at high speed tossing their heads to show spirit. The complete beginner in hand-stitched brogues, standing on his prospective host's feet, and thereby giving a foretaste of what he'll do to the saloon skylight, might even contribute a paper-tearing act. It all needs care. A one-inch forehead is no guarantee of stern reliability and iron resolution any more than a man can be condemned for donning bicycle clips to take the wheel.

Crews have their problems. Artless mention of a new owner may evoke a spasm of pain across listening faces.

'Oh, he's all right,' they'll say, 'as long as you don't take him seriously.'

We have seen this advice in action, the crew standing around smiling gently while the owner gnaws his way through the tiller. Few owners fully appreciate what pain their presence aboard may cause.

Old Harry has no difficulty in finding crews though. Usually they are small men in belted Teddy-bear coats and winkle-pickers who glance constantly over both shoulders and who carry fat black brief cases. They jump ship in Cherbourg and make for Marseilles leaving a trail of thumbprints in tallow and graphite which is followed gratefully by the French Surete.

By tradition an owner completes a weekend spent at the tail of the racing fleet by saying: 'Thank you for a jolly good sail anyway, cheps.'

The crew, following tradition, wave a deprecatory hand and thank him for 'putting up with them'. All scream with laughter at the absurdity of the idea. When they have departed, the owner, grateful to have had such first rate cheps, gets down to the washing up.

Old Harry's Bunkside Book

Make Yourself at Home

THE RELAXED AND easy dispositions of yachtsmen make them natural hosts. Any popular anchorage sees guests massed on one boat or another like ants on an old bone, all climbing in and out of the cockpit with a sausage in one hand and a drink in the other or trying to decide whether to converse under or over the boom. Unfortunately inside an hour the erstwhile mellow evening develops into a raw and rainladen night and nipped and sallow-looking guests yell dutiful conversation above the slapping of halliards.

This athletic aspect of the cocktail party afloat soon breaks down shyness. There can be no lone sentinels brooding over the olives when standing room drives them to a lofty perch on Dorade vent or sheet winch like pole-squatting fakirs.

'Marvellous fun, thanks . . .' they cackle, simulating gaiety as they catch the eye of their host. They windmill desperately to restore balance and thrust the butt of a chipolata into the ear of an elderly stockbroker.

Unlike the good life afloat where conversation never flags, shore entertaining follows a more formal pattern.

'That'll be them!' raps our host as the door bell rings.

'Well, well, well. Come on in and get your things off,' he greets the alert and wary soap salesman on the doorstep. Back in the kitchen our hostess, looking like Mr. Therm in her cherry velvet, is desperately bailing melted Norwegian omelette into the sink and in a frame of mind that would have brought Abdul the terrible Turk to his knees howling for quarter.

From the moment of arrival guests must never be left on their own, otherwise they will either tour the room whistling through their teeth or sit conversing in monotones like trippers in a cathedral. A watch-and-watch system sees our hosts racketing between lounge and kitchen snapping their smiles on and off like music hall comics caught by a faulty curtain.

Old Harry, having a keen interest in interior decoration, needs no entertaining. Prowling the room with critical eye he always has a word of advice for his grateful host.

'Well you've fixed yourself up all right I must say,' he comments winningly, implying ten minutes with some old sacks and a mouthful of tacks, 'but I'd like to pick out your dado for you!'

Old Harry's Bunkside Book

A master of etiquette from the moment he hangs his rowlocks on the hall-stand, Old Harry constitutes a problem for any hostess who prides herself on gay little evenings. Leading in his dinner partner as if teaching her how to use stilts, he seats her and then shoots in her chair with a display of gallantry that wrings forth a gasp of expelled breath and cockbills every candle on the table.

With elbows fanning like some outsize cuckoo fledgling about to quit the nest and save for such brief comments as 'Hello, what's this?' and 'Ah that's better' which mark the arrival and departure of dishes, he is a silent guest at table. The more so since hostesses these days consider a meal skimped unless it is difficult to eat. If they can't stuff it they must serve it on a skewer.

'Hah! Pump washers on a fid eh!' laughs Harry with a rare flash of wit as he slides mushrooms off the spit and into the lap of his neighbour. Haggard hostesses watch him fake and snake his spaghetti in seamanly fashion the better to ensure free-running coils as he sucks it home. They duck instinctively as the bitter end whips free and vanishes in a spray of gravy.

A meal as a guest of Old Harry is another matter. Setting his pressure cooker in the centre of the table and releasing the steam in a billowing cloud which draws a merciful cloak across the scene for a few brief moments, he lifts the lid and begins poking around inside as if looking for a lost stop-cock. Each guest gazes in fascination as he receives one blue potato and a tremulous gobbet of mutton.

'There's plenty — don't be frightened of it'. Harry reassures, sorting them round on the plates like some geologist cataloguing fossils.

'There's nothing wasted with pressure cookers' he declares, fishing out an unidentifiable fragment and lobbing it back hastily.

Fitting Out and Laying Up

THE MID-FITTING OUT cocktail party is my particular dread. 'We'll just put in an appearance' your wife says, hinting at a quick leap into the centre of the floor to a chorus of horrified gasps. Once you're in among the cheese-dippers you are lost. 'It's been lovely' you lie, inching doorwards. Your wife has her lips shut tighter than a nunnery back window. The rest of fitting out is fine and I love it. You never seem to finish in time of course and the boat next door is always ready before you. 'They're putting me in next Thursday' the owner confides. You muse darkly about an all-together-now heave and a flailing owner plummeting off the end of the jetty.

Not a Patch On It

YOU DON'T REALISE how filthy your sails have become until you see the sailmaker lay them out in the loft. He unrolls them with the distaste of a four-star hotel chambermaid laying out chain-store pyjamas. Ignoring the track of Magister footprints leading from leech to luff and the variegated blotching that makes them look like disused pantomime scenery, he walks round the outside with exaggerated ceremony. It's cut he's interested in.

'You've got a nasty little belly,' he comments pointedly.

The owner-sailmaker relationship tends to be a bit guarded. No sail is really right until it is worn out, say owners discouragingly. The sailmaker, knowing what he has set out to produce, is gloomily prepared to see his customer back on Monday complete with bundle and scowl.

The housewife with a Food-of-all-nations cookery book, a green pepper and a sack of rice is in a similar position.

'It's called *pasti*,' she explains unhelpfully as she lifts the tailboard and stacks the old man's plate.

She waits with grim resignation while the hub of her little universe,

Old Harry's Bunkside Book

jaws champing like a stone-crusher, pauses to jerk out his verdict.

The sailmaker, working to the baffling instructions of an owner who has graduated from a converted assault boat and has just read 'Offshore', embarks upon his task without illusion and eventually sends in his bill with the optimism of a poet submitting verse to the 'Poultry Gazette'. Owners work on the assumption that their sailmaker can take neither rest nor nourishment until the sail is cut to perfection. Their arrival back with imaginery imperfections makes them as popular as a doorstep theologian on washday.

'I think we'll have to have another look at this leech,' they laugh.

The craftsman, arising from his nest on the floor with the stoical resignation of a basset hound caught in the linen basket shambles forward with a black heart. An uninvited wedding guest opening his postal box of cake crumbs has been known to exhibit more unrestrained delight than the sailmaker unrolling a sail for the fourth time — he has only to make some more pencil marks on it, roll it up in a tight wad with some bent eyelets and send it back in order to win the gratified approval of his client.

The bespoke tailor putting tape to paunch in the realization that only a pair of braces like cargo hooks will check such pants in their crashing descent is on a safer bet than the sailmaker facing a dinghy man hot from a Continental season. Bubbling over about rule-cheating cuts and cloths which run in more odd directions than a barnyard hen with a worm, he makes heavy demands on the traditionalist who is accustomed to working out problems on the back of a fag-packet.

Old Harry carries out his own repairs. Periodical whoops of startled agony demonstrate his mastery of the flat-hand technique in seaming and drama is added with the discovery that his jib has become an integral part of his fearnaughts. He only patronises his sailmaker for new sails or repairs of hopeless complexity.

'Here you are then,' he says generously. 'You can do a job of cobbling on this for me.'

He offers a set of boltropes fringed with salt-blasted remnants of sail. The consultation which follows, conducted largely in grunts of mutual distrust would daunt a lesser man than Harry.

'I can't look at the job,' raps the sailmaker, looking at it in awed fascination. He eventually undertakes the work as his only defence against the permanent presence of Harry, stationed by the coke bogy.

On the rare occasions when Old Harry needs a new sail, even such a traditionalist as his sailmaker is daunted. Presiding in person from start to finish, gathering up offcuts with jealous hand and eyelets with practised flick of the boot, Harry gleans the floor bare as a birdtable in winter. The traditional sailmaker's dislike of being watched at work is dismissed with lively good humour. Resting a toe on the bench Harry plies his glowering craftsman with helpful tip and wrinkle.

The old-time cotton man, raised in the art of putting in wrinkles for the owner to get out, finds himself nowhere with Harry's sails. Those great tan pelts which you couldn't stretch even with a stump-puller defy even Harry's efforts but the ceremony of stretching a new sail is still a time of crisis. If you netted five pounds for improper use of leech line you'd be in the chips. Reaching back and forth across the river, applying tension to that great shimmying sack, with the nervy concentration of a novice fiddler tuning by ear and already two octaves sharp, he sets a novel problem for racing fleets concerned about rights of way.

Harry's sailmaker, last of a line of men who could cut and seam a barge mainsail over their knees and belt in a cringle liner at one go without swallowing their chaw, makes no concessions to the client.

Nerved to face that pendant lower lip the owner must make his approach to the loft with such pitiful show of authority as he can screw up. The door, self-shutting by reason of a two-inch joining shackle on a pulley, reduces his attempt at dignified and leisurely entry to a grunting scuffle followed at once by a ringing slap that propels him on-stage like a reluctant Sunbeam at a school concert. A baleful glare greets this cheerful entry and a dusty silence settles down again.

Only after our owner has studied a 1935 trade calendar depicting gaff-rigged mayhem on the Clyde and cautiously captioned 'Getting their gun', whistled gems from Faust with drummed-finger accompaniment and cleared his throat like some guest speaker trying to break the uncanny silence which followed his joke will the sailmaker show signs of offering service.

'I can't look at it!' he states flatly.

Let All the Family Help

IT WOULD BE fascinating (if useless) to know just how far the yachtsman walks backwards in admiration of his topsides at this time of year.

'She hasn't come up badly,' he affirms modestly, bending with effort, to squint at her from between his knees. 'Mind you,' he continues, unaware that his original audience has been replaced by a police constable attracted to the scene by mingled doubt and duty, Mind you my bottom hasn't come up properly yet, not by a long way.'

The annual application of paint is hailed as a laughing frolic in the sun by the paint manufacturer. He supplies little cut-out yachts with his colour cards as a spur to the boggling imaginations of owners, who flit from 'Eau-de-nil' and 'Buff' back to 'Tropic Blue' with the mounting desperation of worker bees right out of pollen and doing the rounds of the plastic mimosa

Old Harry's Bunkside Book

with a half-hour to go to sunset.

'What do you reckon she'd look like in "Dawn Flight Pink"?' queries our worried owner, peering through his cut-out like a prisoner at the grill. His converted lifeboat, with a wheel-house like a confessional on a handcart, would acquire the sort of distinction accorded to a stray Liberty Bodice in an Yves St. Laurent Spring Collection.

Despite the popular belief that "This new stuff will stand up to anything you care to do to it', the mystique attached to applying paint dies hard. Let your drama student look to the yachtsman for an exposition of sheer naked emotion. Just let him get half-way along his topsides with the old epoxy when the first drop of rain falls. He can't believe it at first and gives a shrill, mad laugh.

'I thought for a moment it was raining!' he mutters wildly, taking a fresh dip in the pot. No courtier in mid-bow noting the bounding flight of a trouser button across the parquet, could straighten up in greater haste than our man upon feeling the second cooling droplet. The emotions chase one another across his face like an Operatic Society Figaro working up steam for the sob sequence.

Painting holds no terrors for Old Harry. Cherishing no brief for any paint that isn't pure lead and which can be lifted with one hand, the Workhouse Brown and Town Hall Green of his present colour scheme puts him down an inch on his marks per coat. Prior to the acquisition of his present stocks – a nocturnal cash encounter with a man with close-set eyes and narrow nostrils – he had hitherto mixed his own paint. Applied with bucket and Long Tom, this healthy nostrum had amazing coverage and returning owners of neighbouring craft – like motorists meeting a milkvan approaching backwards on the wrong side of the road – greet their speckled topsides with cries of rueful laughter.

It is an over-rated pastime in any case. 'Let all the family help!' jeer the You-Do-It-Yourself-Then articles, goading an already harassed owner. We have seen this loveless little scene – young helpers armed with brushes of oak-like solidity hopelessly rapping their way along the ballast keel like convicts seeking some faint means of communication while mother savagely annoints soft rolls with hard butter using a penknife and frozen fingers.

Father meanwhile has started his topsides with dedicated care. Unlike Old Harry who prepares for painting by doing a quick circuit swiping off barnacles with his cap, our man has rubbed, filled and primed to perfection. Laying on enamel with a new brush and undaunted by the acreage ahead or the sudden dribbles of water that snake down from each deck scupper in turn as he passes it, he works on with the plodding devotion of a master mason starting work on a cathedral. Somewhere along the line comes a dramatic change. By dusk he is slapping paint over the rudder pintles as if he were disinfecting a fowl-house. His wife is waiting in the car with her jaw set like an Easter Island statue and the kids, having whined their way into back-seat incarceration, have begun unravelling their jumper sleeves – a preliminary to the belt round the ear which rounds off yet another day of healthy fun in the open air.

Old Harry's Bunkside Book

The Finishing Touch

IT WAS A dark day for the neighbours at fitting out time when Old Harry discovered roller-painting. As far as science concerns him Faraday might just as well have gone up with his kite but the modern roller method wins his full approval. Armed with a dripping juggernaut cleverly contrived from rolling pin and hearth-rug he thunders round his topsides leaving a broad swathe that clears bystanders like a motor mower flushing courting couples from a municipal golf course. Let some poor fellow get too close and he wins himself a gas-house tar cummerbund and a boot-top of tallow and sheep-dip.

Old Harry's homely techniques call for a certain amount of criticism in the close confines of the yard. He can raise more dust than Moses quitting Egypt. If he shakes his blankets there are beautiful sunsets for a fortnight. Rubbing down, an operation calling for a paper so coarse that it has to be sold under the counter, is always accompanied by a harsh hissing sound common to ostlers frooming livery nags. It raises a swirling dust that settles like a Japanese snowstorm in a bottle. Woe to the owner who arrives at the yard resolved to put on his final enamel.

'Actually I *had* planned to put on my top-coat today', he says loudly, enunciating with careful clarity and peering through the gloom. Old Harry, glancing at the sky, nods his approval of this decision and begins dusting down the deck with his cap. Not even when he is doing his own painting is there any guarantee of success for others. Sighting a gratified eye along the lunar landscape of his topsides he presses a vast melton rump firmly up against the fresh enamel of the neighbouring hull.

No bird building its nest in a factory hooter shows more misguided optimism than the owner in the matter of his topside enamel. Below water the finish may have as much lustre as a nightwatchman's waistcoat. You could grate cheese on his garboards and hang your cap on his hood ends but above the waterline an undulating gloss speaks of trembling brush-hand and hushed figures tip-toeing round like gas-fitters in a nunnery. Two months later we find the owner in his dinghy making a mournful pilgrimage round his battered topsides, which have been hammered into more dents than a factory-Tudor sideboard.

'Just look at this one!' he sobs.

However, painting is only a small part of fitting out. When it comes to

Old Harry's Bunkside Book

rubbing down, our owner shies clear, wisely harbouring his special talents for more intricate work.

'Don't be afraid of using sandpaper' he encourages, eyeing his muttering team with expansive generosity. Let them waste a piece though . . .

'Who threw THIS away?' he falters brokenly. He holds up a soggy fragment for inspection, his expressions altering rapidly from laughing optimism to beaten resignation like a picture ad. prophesying life without an endowment policy. He demonstrates the fine abrasive qualities remaining in it, rubbing with a brief vigour which would shift boiler scale with a *papier poudre.*

Work aloft on a sunny day ('I'm not going to ask anyone else to go UP THERE') sees him giving of his best. Like a gardener intrigued by the hectic life beneath the lifted stone he watches his crew scuttle about the deck below at his bidding. The omnipotent smirk would snap off his face if he could see Blanche's boy turning up his gantline on the burgee cleat ('Uncle's life is in your hands lad') but from up there the moronic fumbling in search of block and shackle pin make him drunk with power. The pale upturned faces flanked by feet and foreshortened by height look like middle-aged cherubim taxiing for take-off.

Turning the engine over is another little chore calling for the accumulated skill of ownership.

'There's no reason why she shouldn't start' he reasons, rising from the handle with scarlet face and dewy brow. The dutiful little Greek chorus of side-kicks who stand ready with sympathy on these occasions cluck helpfully in time with his grunts of strain.

'She fired!' they cheer without conviction as his knuckles thud into the woodwork. When she does fire it is with startling suddenness. Father has been easing open the throttle by degrees. The engine explodes into life with a screaming whoop, exhaust blasting a salvo of soot and spiders, and dancing a mad tarantella on its bearers.

'Short her, short her!' he howls fumbling with the dismantled switch. Seizing the screwdriver he claps it across the plug leads before a con-rod can boot its way through the casing. The health-giving high tension shock jerks him to attention like a liberty-boat matelot denying all knowledge of the tobacco warehouse revealed in his cap.

Old Harry's Bunkside Book

It's Hardly Fitting

AROUND THE YARDS winter covers are being rolled back and owners, contemplating the cardboard boxes of rusty rigging and the rich toupee worn by the frying pan, are wondering how they can contrive to disguise in fitting out the fact that they didn't actually lay up.

The rip-out is the answer. Rip out the whole accommodation and put back again like shaking the dog's bed. Later — and catching your eye as it feasts upon a row of halving joints that look like the Devil's Causeway, they beg your indulgence.

'I'm afraid we had to do a rush job this year,' they apologise, implying that given time they could make Chippendale look like a home handyman.

Denied plumb-bob and spirit level, the yachtsman must work by eye — a process which rewards him with enough sawdust to stock a circus and a galley drawer which has to be prised open with a fork.

'It'll get easier in time' he forecasts optimistically as he somersaults backwards with the rich chuckle occasioned by a pickle fork up his trumpet.

The bolt on the inside of the heads door which never quite shoots home (watched by an alert and anxious inmate) is another product of the calculating eye.

All over the country, yachtsmen are lifting the lids of their tool boxes — an abortive move this since the tools have long-since been absorbed into kitchen dresser and attic or suspended on little racks in the shed from which they drop like a stick of bombs everytime you slam the door.

Nevertheless there is the handsaw, aptly named since the owner must force its shuddering passage through the plank with both fists and a well-placed boot. The tenon saw, embedded after two strokes like King Arthur's sword and the pad-saw which has to be straightened out before use like a carnival nose, complete his main armoury. Cutting tools, on the other hand, are nearer to his heart. The plane, fresh from the ironmonger and its annual sharpen-up encourages him to all manner of exquisite work and the illusion of working with a keen edge persists long after the stage has been reached when each lunge raises a jagged weal which couldn't be bettered using a mace. Only when the tool is stuffed solid with splinters, gorged to repletion, is it laid aside with a sigh.

Old Harry's Bunkside Book

Old Harry, who fancies his arm with the adze, is given a clear field by neighbouring yachtsmen. He owns the only vessel I know with battlements and a foredeck like a clock-golf course. His offer to 'Dub your topsides smooth as a china jug' is met with the hasty headshake. The hornet whine of flying chips, each the size of a young pullet, tells its own tale and the toe-caps of his seaboots, severed during earlier fitouts are rapidly becoming prized collector's pieces by antiquarians.

The vogue for building boats from old wardrobes has hit the auction rooms with a surge of new prosperity. Hunters of Victoriana have to be hot off the pedals to beat your boatbuilder. The keen bidder, seated in his wardrobe rowing reflectively with a pair of fire-irons while he awaits the hammer is fast becoming a familiar sight.

As a source of material for below-deck alterations the wardrobe is unmatched and there is many a cabin door with built-in trouser press and sturdy coachroof beams lettered 'Strand Palace Hotel'!

Down in the timber yards where leather-padded maties, swift of foot, double round and round the stacks merrily evading the customer, we find the yachtsman (with his chitty from the office for six foot of 1 x 1½in. pine) in full command of the situation. Yard foremen in cloth caps powdered like a shop bun, quail before his expert knowledge.

'Why yes sir' they laugh, fanning their forelocks, 'of course I can cut that little straight piece out of the middle of the plank'. Their voices tremble with eagerness to please.

Old Harry is not the man to be fobbed off with a stick of deal studded with knots like a Garibaldi biscuit and more shakes per foot than a wet dog. I remember him showing me how to buy teak. The test, it seemed, was to bring the butt of your plank down to earth with a hearty thud whereupon it should ring like a bell. He applied this revealing test at once whereupon the yard foreman went bounding off up the yard on one foot uttering tremendous roars of approbation for this show of skill.

NO MATTER HOW often we start the fit-out wearing rubber gloves, we end up lying prone, with cheek pressed against the cabin sole, prodding out a limber hole with a finger that looks as though it belongs on the herbalist's shelves. There is no substitute for bare hands. We begin overhauling the heads with delicate and shrinking touch, poking around with bits of

Old Harry's Bunkside Book

stick and end up with rolled sleeves, squared jaw and old traitor toothpaste tube cap held aloft to the chastened family between finger and thumb; damning evidence of wilful neglect. We get the same knife, fork and spoon for the next three days.

The medical profession, strangely addicted to cruising, carries the stigma of fitting out into its clinical world. The patient, who has dined without pleasure on barium meal in readiness for examination, submits to the prodding with scant confidence. 'Do we feel any discomfort here... or here?' queries the medic poking away with a Kobe green finger.

Sunday evening bathroom sessions with father grinding away at the pumice, treat back door visitors to a view of the bathwater and, being unable to identify antifouling when they see it, they depart in haste from that livid flood leaving the gate open.

Official receptions held around this time of year can prove a strain. Your yachtsman in his dinner jacket, struggling to hold a glass with his knuckles in order to hide his nails is a sight to evoke pity. 'Poor devil' people mutter, trying not to look at him, 'it makes you thankful doesn't it.' A dinner, with a score or so of yachtsmen trying to hold fish knives as if about to beat a tattoo and a Principal Guest rendered waggish by a patch of Polyurethane one-can on the lobe of his left ear becomes a nightmare for the social photographer.

Any hostess anxious for a fine day for her Spring midday Sunday cocktail party only needs to invite a few cruiser owners to be assured of a windless and brilliantly sunny day with the first skylark carolling on high; she'll also get a little knot of angry men in a corner near the window, looking at their watches and exchanging comments from the sides of their mouths.

The mid-fitout cocktail party ('Don't take your coat off Margaret, we'll be out of this lot by 1 o'clock') is about as ill advised as a silver collection for the Dumb Friends League at 2 am in a tom-cat haunted neighbourhood. Yachtsmen are drawn away from their boats as if by some nightmare Kraken.

They'll need just another 5 minutes to finish cutting in the cove line. 'God — look at the time' instructs father profanely; he dashes for home and with kick-off at 12.30 he thunders in at 12.25, boilersuited, booted and with a wagging sticking plaster on one finger — a Bengal Lancer charging hopeless odds.

His wife will be ready and waiting in a figure-flattering little dress that looks as if she'd lagged herself from neck to knee with insulating tape. She's up on her heels and down at the mouth corners, made up with artistry and powdered like a cream bun. 'Well *really*', she flutes, 'have you *any* idea of the time'. A stickler for sensible information he tells her and wins himself a frizzing.

Barrier cream is about as effective as a parlourmaid's apron. Eventually, when the hands are washed, all superficial dirt dissolves leaving them looking like a political map of troubled Europe, finger tips etched with black like a row of nuns in a choir stall. Any hand-cream not containing turps, Vim and Bilgex is doomed to failure but the blackest of hands are little white doves by comparison to Old Harry's claws.

Old Harry's Bunkside Book

Even at normal times they would disturb the fastidious. At fitting out time the smearing, stirring, poking and digging, the mixing of unguents beneficial to oak and hemp, the probing of inky mysteries in pumpwell and sump and the exploratory gropings around mooring roots give his hands alien personalities of their own. His genial 'Let me give you a hand' to neighbouring yachtsmen takes on a gruesome implication. Shopkeepers push his change at him across the counter as if feeding a tarantula and, raised in greeting, short-sighted bird-lovers have been known to throw crumbs to it. On the social scene Old Harry's hand, offered once in greeting to a sensitive lady of nervous nature invited disaster. Shot from his cuff like a horned toad emerging from its hateful lair it brought a broken cry to her lips and she staggered back grasping her stuffed olives. Old Harry, quick to sense her discomfort, put her at ease with honeyed word.

'Keep away from the volly vonts' he confided, leaning close, 'or you'll likely get a riding turn in your top set.'

THE PRIVATE LOCK-UP store tenanted throughout the winter by a crafty-eyed old professional is almost a thing of the past. Nowadays your owner is stuck with his gear.

' 'These sails are a capital asset', he snarls over his shoulder as he battles upstairs with his mottled treasures. It's not until mother goes to her wardrobe to take down her little maroon two-piece and finds his number two jib with its hanks enmeshed in her mohair like a falcon starting in on an old pullet, that the dogs of war are really unleashed.

That hopeless cry.

'I'm going to make a bit of room in my shed' is without substance.

He fingers through his boxes of pinless shackles, bits of gas pipe and odd rowlocks in the periodical turn-out and ends by rejecting (after long deliberation) a brick-hard antifouling brush wrapped in an old shirt and two old Aerolite kits which are all acid and no gum. The rest goes back.

Old Harry has a shed so packed with handy gear that entry is only practicable when he is stocktaking. At other times he is to be seen shading his eyes at the window, gloating over his wares and speculating on the wide range of exigencies which might be met by the imaginative use of mangle handle or barbola picture frame.

Old Harry's Bunkside Book

Gear which has stewed in a dank locker throughout a wet summer and grown a fur coat that couldn't be bettered by the Hudson Bay Company must — feels our owner — be cosseted throughout the winter. While mother is pouring tea for the Young Wives ('I'm not one to criticise, but I don't know *what* he sees in her . . .') a series of booming thuds overhead sets her plastic brilliants rattling. The taut smile and an explanation that it's only Norman in the false roof is tardy consolation to a lady who has a powdering of ceiling plaster like a shop bun.

The black and tentacled shape of a magneto crouching among the guest towels in the airing cupboard is another source of laughing remonstrance. It is not without hazard though. A harsh cry of

'Frank! Frank! Get the aerosol', accompanied by brutal attack with a bath-brush can ruin a man's timing.

One largely unexplored domestic territory is to be found beneath the bed. Here and there a wife may meet with resistance as she probes beneath it with her vacuum cleaner, possibly sucking up ten fathoms of 16-plait before she can hit the switch, but old Harry is one of the few men we know who has exploited this area to full advantage.

The unexpected guest, full of brown ale and basking in the warmth of his host's hospitality goes unwittingly to his doom.

'I hope you've got everything you need', Harry intones formally as he nudges his guest through the door before he can make for the bathroom.

It is a hope which would be well-founded if an extended cruise was intended. With a grateful sigh our man hurls himself upon the suspiciously mountainous mattress. There is a jangle like the start of a dray-horse Derby drowned by his bellow of outraged pain as he meets the fluke of a forty-pound Nicholson. He spends the rest of the night trying to arrange a nest for his hip between throat halliard blocks and binnacle.

Nor is your dinghy man free of worries. Don't send your sails to the laundry, plead a dozen yachting writers in peevish harmony each autumn. The cry goes unheeded. Laundry managers settling to their correspondence and the Monday morning apologia for missing dickies and shirts with battle-banner tails, read with dismay that Mrs. Plackett of 'Bon Jardin' has entered the maternity ward well kitted out with a 190 sq.ft. nighty bearing the confusing legend FO 93. Somewhere else a dinghy man will be furrowing his brow over a spinnaker with a plunging neckline.

The conveyance of gear from lay-up to home sees some grim little safaris. No Easter Week penitent in old Seville was ever more thoroughly hooded than your owner weaving along the seawall with two settee mattresses on his head. Mother, bringing up the rear, being better equipped by nature for this and trousered like Coco, the laughable clown, carries the misleading label 'Fairy Snow' on her carton of assorted galley ware.

The drive home from the yard is not without a certain passing interest. With the boot half open on a speckled sail-bag like some luckless monster gagging on a railway pasty and the back seats stacked to the roof with implements of navigation the back of the chassis drags the road like a well-nourished fat-tail sheep.

Mother, nursing her box, doubles as a rear-view mirror with a tart com-

Old Harry's Bunkside Book

mentary on the queue of laughing drivers astern. With faithful Percy next to the driver and trying to keep a propeller on his lap while fielding his end of the oars clear of the gear lever it is only a matter of time . . . Father, approaching the traffic lights, brakes, de-clutches and hauls his burgee stick aft into second. Bus-drivers give him a sporting cheer as he goes bounding over the line in top pursued by Reeds Nautical Almanac and a scattering of lentils.

Dress

I HAVE NEVER understood how other men manage to wear cravats and towelling scarves without looking like vultures around the neck. It's the same with Proper Yachting Caps. I seldom wear one but when I do it either rises high on my scalp and looks like a scatter cushion or a ruse to improve my deportment or I cram it hard down and my eyebrows are raised like a martyr at the stake. Neither can I wander around the boat in my pyjamas the way other men do. Mine always *gape*. I may stick my head and shoulders out of the hatch when the Harbour Master's launch comes alongside, secure in the belief that I am decent, only to find his young nipper staring in fascination through the coachroof window lower down.

Well Turned Out

'I TAKE IT you'll be wearing your reefer,' croaks the yachting wife without enthusiasm. Her young married ambition to get him into a tail suit ('Of course he's tall with it you know') was stifled at a very early date. The lure of the glossy dicky has no hold on your reefer man.

A room filled with yachtsmen all looking like labradors is no riot of gay colour perhaps, but the well-cut reefer presents an impeccable sight above the waist – what happens below it – the tapering off into venerable flannels with kneecaps like twin loving cups concerns no-one at a well-packed function.

We're not talking of your off-the-peg wonderful values with décolleté neckline that leaves the leathery-necked man looking like a turkey coming out of a basket, nor the slack skirt like a safety curtain for that matter which envelopes the chair-back upon sitting down and imparts a false military air to the wearer at table! No, a 'made-to-measure' reefer is essential.

Probably one of the most fascinating of all sights is the yachtsman in the sanctity of his bathroom completing a self-measurement form for a new postal offer. He has a diagram of a yachtsman, quartered like a bullock and trussed with dotted lines showing, somewhat unnecessarily, how to crook the elbow. Our man, torn between pride and precision, doesn't know whether to expand his chest and produce a gratifyingly husky measurement which will net him a fit like a stick of garden rhubarb in an upturned bucket or give 'chest normal' and all it implies and end up with a reefer that makes him look like an out-of-service parking meter.

'I like a loose fit so I can wear a thick sweater,' he claims later, hunching his shoulders.

Once properly fitted the illusion of being well-dressed persists long beyond the stage when buttons swing on pendant thread like egg-sexers and the wallet dropped carelessly into an inside pocket plummets to the bottom of the lining. It matters little that other pockets are rich with a loam of fluff and tobacco dust while access to the lower lining, via a hole punctured by a copper nail permits the wearer to grope thoughtfully among long-lost treasures. Cut is all that matters.

It's a bold man, though, who'll produce a handful of small change without turning decently aside to sort fluff. I've seen them sorting it on a counter under the barman's level stare, struggling to maintain that eerie smile through a variety of facial contortions reminiscent of a piano accordionist knocking off arpeggios with an eye to the clock. Then there are those among us who, helped into our reefers by washroom attendant, have plunged an arm deep into the lining. With a wretched little laugh we wrench it out only to find that it is swaddled in some form of sacking.

It's not so easy to take your reefer to sea and still maintain that pristine loveliness.

'Wait until it dries and then that stuff will brush off,' is hollow comfort to the man who has to roll his sleeve up and grapple. No matter how far he shoves it up, there comes the moment when it shoots down with the speed of a striking snake.

The cruising owner, ripe for a run ashore, has no illusions. No sooner has he changed and wandered on deck to wait for Mabel (who is still trying to get both elbows into the plastic bowl) than the tide turns and he finds himself gazing into the nostrils of the man astern. Mabel, all headscarf, box-pleats and eye-shadow, will be in nice time to tail on to the anchor chain. Later, dining ashore by candlelight, all eyes are on the healthy couple.

Mabel is wearing her eye-shadow as if she'd just gone ten rounds with a welter. The waiter flicks manfully at a stray mollusc and tries to say 'huîtres marinées' with his lips pursed.

The British yachtsman on foreign soil is not hard to distinguish. His doeskin is stabbed by the envious glances of those who must wear reefers which are either too blue or cut like a Cinzano bottle. Not even the Italians who have given us vertical stripes or the Americans who pulled out our shirts, cut off the tails and peppered our paunches with palm trees can detract from our reefer.

Old Harry, in an historic reefer which buttons to his glottis and a cap which originated above the thunderous brow of a Schools Crossings Officer, can hold his own in the best-dressed Continental circles. Elbowing his way to the bar with the firm though not unfriendly vigour which once built an empire he is soon the centre of interest as awed Common Marketeers take in the rich and paint-encrusted patina of cuff and lapel.

Old Harry's Bunkside Book

Always ready to shake the hand across the sea, I have seen him turn on his nearest admirer and taking a fold of the poor fellow's jacket between finger and thumb, demonstrate its lack of tensile strength convincingly — and in the very highest of British good humour.

Knit One, Purl One

IF THERE IS one thing that upsets a sailing man it's the threat of washing his sweater.

'You'd better let me run it through for you,' notes his wife distastefully, implying that she'll handle it with a stick. Recalling the inky effluent that gushed from the sink drain under the nervous eye of the postman on the last occasion, she doesn't press the point.

This reluctance to surrender his pelt to the dramatic reincarnation promised by the detergent manufacturers stems from the twin fears that it will on the one hand be robbed of its natural oils and the other be transformed in size and shape.

We have seen men gazing down in panic at their exposed and cringing abdomens while trying vainly to drag at a shrunken hem with hands muffled in a two-foot surplus of sleeve. Others, encased from neck to knee in a woollen tube lack only a cloche hat and a string of amber beads.

As a third alternative a man's sweater may shrink evenly and uncannily to accommodate a thirty-four inch bust, whereupon he next sees it worn with a headscarf and box pleats.

'I'll knit you a nice one for your birthday,' consoles Norah ignoring his sudden spasm of dread. She produces a pattern picturing a man smoking an empty pipe and taking a sun sight on Oulton Broad.

'Ahoy there!' it commands, 'a woolly to knit for the sea-going HIM in your life.'

This sunny prospect is to haunt him for weeks to come. He watches it take shape under the flying needles with the dumb fascination of a biologist observing some new and terrible mutation. At intervals he stands with shoulders hunched while a multihued tabard is draped over his front and back for feminine consultation.

'I wish I'd cast off 4 sts. at beg last rw.' she muses, tugging at a castellated hem. His first emergence in full glory sporting a pattern like a seismic

Old Harry's Bunkside Book

graph sees him moving at a rapid shuffle from doorway to doorway, eyes baleful with challenge for the passer-by.

At the club he meets his greatest test. No hospital patient babbles his explanation of the water bed's eerie rumbles and squelches more urgently than does the new owner of a sea-horse bedecked sweater confronted by the poker-faced scrutiny of his fellow members. His attempts to dull the heraldic magnificence by groping under the bilge for gas bottle spanner or shackle meet with stern rebuke.

The plain navy sweater may be about as much fun to knit as a fire-hose but the illusion of sober neatness persists long after the polo-neck has sagged to a lei of grubby ribbing and the body has assumed a muffin-bell contour — a deception heightened by the clapper-like effect of knicker and knee-cap.

Left to his own devices a man will buy his sweaters at the yachting outfitter, scuttling off with the first they show him (too short in the arm) rather than be coaxed into a changing cubicle with its aura of stuffy intimacy. Alternatively he patronises the surplus stores where the jaded fruits of fire, war and bankruptcy are laid out for his approval. A squat little man with a fore and aft trouser measurement like a dirigible starved of helium, offers an astounding bargain which contains about as much wool as a pauper's shroud and which cannot be repeated. It will let the wind through like the seventh veil and offers no more warmth than a shower curtain.

Old Harry, who, when dressed for sea would make the wool-sack look like a raffia place mat, is haunted by the flock of naked and tight-lipped sheep which contributed to his present fleecy prize. Presented by a compassionate and zealous worker for Seamen's Relief, who found him in his long-johns searching for his trousers after the fitting out supper, it was originally begun as a frock by an unknown Dagenham spinster with a figure like a Henry Moore bronze. Having used the wrong needles and proceeded in st.sts. instead of K.1 P.1 she added a roll neck and heaved it out with the pious hope that 'some poor soul may be glad of it.'

Harry has scorned the wash-tub since the regrettable time when he took a sweater to the laundrette. The window of the machine offered a sight which drew staff and patrons alike to witness what appeared to be the death throes of a giant squid. Labouring under the final spin it quitted the ranks and strutted out into the street where Old Harry cornered it and forced it to give up its prey. Watchers bit their lips and turned aside as his trembling fingers held up what appeared to be a tea-cosy.

Old Harry's Bunkside Book

I Find It a Dreadful Tie

CLUB TIES ARE generally praiseworthy for their restraint. There are ordinary ties which are of such colourful glory that the sternum appears to be ablaze from belt to glottis; others, while less tropical, are embellished with the sort of pattern which looks like an unfortunate accident with the porridge. The dark blue club tie with its sprinkling of modest burgees merely offers a challenge to short-sighted and compulsive fluff-pickers. *New* club ties are another matter.

The newly elected club member, basking under the accolade of his new tie and wearing it spread across his chest like a heraldic tabard, is not long in realising that something is wrong. The glossy ostentation of it would make your costly mink wrap look like a cow-man's ferret.

The healthy patina of a veteran tie is not acquired easily. Like the annular rings of the sturdy oak tree each layer and stain records history. No matter that it lies there with the limp unloveliness of an unrolled cocktail anchovy, it has survived a score of Men's Nights and been mangled in with the genoa sheet in a riding turn that split the night with its wearer's falsetto howls.

Club regalia as a whole is not to be dismissed lightly. The term is misleading. One tends to associate it with the glittering showcase, electronic burglar traps and Beefeaters rankling under the merry gaze of American tourists. *Club* regalia, on the other hand, is more likely to be cached in a brown paper bag under the bar, presided over by the steward and demanded at rare intervals by members. The prices of individual goodies are none the less awe-inspiring.

'How much would this one be?' queries a member holding up a burgee the size of dolly's bib.

'It works out at 37s 6d,' offers the steward, working it out. The member, dropping it with haste and an unreciprocated attempt at mirth, chooses a still smaller one (which might have been the better for a gummed backing) and parts with fifteen bob like an evicted tenant bidding farewell to Old Dobbin.

The club tie is important in establishing a man's maritime status. It should be noted though that the student who hauls out a man's tie for scrutiny, as if reading a ticker-tape, may win a whistle of displeasure from

Old Harry's Bunkside Book

the stately nostrils of a Founder Member. More appropriate than the detailed examination with narrowed eyes and hands on bended knees, is the quick flick of the eye — the gaze turned aside decently as if noting old traitor cornflake stuck to unwitting chin.

Old Harry, a veteran clubman, who has severed some diplomatic ties in his time, boasts a collection of these abbreviated relics. Souvenirs of last-man-in-the-bar and unsteady exits under the steward's steady eye, they date back to the era of the cardboard dicky and the reefing bowsprit.

Having received the regrets of every House Committee on the coast and collected enough black balls to stuff a sofa, he has (pending the formation of some more clubs) been forced to devise his own club and tie. This astonishing garment, cleverly contrived from a spare Rippingill wick and featuring a motif of crossed bilge pumps on a gum-boot, is the insignia of the Upper Tannery Creek SC, Commodore, Hon Sec and Hon Treasurer Old Harry.

On the last occasion of his visit to Cowes Week (neaped on the Squadron steps) this tie excited the attention of an astounded doeskin audience but an otherwise successful debut on the social scene had an unfortunate conclusion.

Acquiring a ticket to a reception of note, he made a stately entrance, tore it in half for the doorman, tipped the MC and advanced upon his hostess. Leaning well forward to kiss her hand, his tie fell foul of her Pimms Number One. It mopped up that beverage like a purser's sponge cake in a puddle and had started work on the fruit before its wearer became alert to this crisis. Reacting with typical old world charm he shot his cuffs and had wrung it out into her glass again before she could murmur her thanks.

Navigation

There are navigators who can make the tiniest of crosses on their charts and who cover jotting pads with columns of neat and meaningful figures. I jot on anything handy. My fixes on the chart look like ducks' feet. I put my arm over it when people walk past. I don't credit my running fixes and that Monster Fun Book, the tidal atlas, has my landfalls anywhere that you least expect them, like moles on a lawn.

A Spell with the Bottles

'SOMEBODY MUST TRY to win this race,' the owner says, waving aside food and sleep.

He thrusts his unshaven muzzle up into the cockpit, taking in the following breeze and close-hauled genoa.

'Oh,' he pleads, using his special Little Lord Fauntleroy voice, 'Please don't anybody move . . . I . . . I think I can manage to set the spinnaker alone.'

The watch, which has been grunting and straining in the cockpit like a litter of over-size pups in an undersize basket for the past four hours of light variables, begins to rush around in a savage burlesque of efficiency. This is the moment when Percy, on his first offshore race, chooses to quit his bunk for the first time and wing his way up on deck in shorts and shirt tails.

'I think I'll feel better on deck,' he confides to the birds.

His worries are at an end. He has just booked himself for a session with the bottles.

On most offshore buckets at some time or other we can study these windswept figureheads, straining forward, binoculars clapped to uncaring eye, salty little sentinels forever gazing in search of sail numbers. Earlier perhaps they were splitting at the seams in their efforts to do such right things as frowning when everybody else frowned and examining the genoa luff with the carefully composed expression of intelligent inquiry of an art mistress in the Tate Gallery. Wounded perhaps by a long and draughty exile on the weather sidedeck ('where your weight will do some good at least,') they take to the pulpit as though it was some sudden and gratifying

Old Harry's Bunkside Book

promotion. The world they watch through the 12 x 50's is a dizzy welter in which huge objects swoop to and fro like staff nurses ejecting visitors.

The navigator will have long since explained things if there should be a total absence of competing craft. It will be the proof of the success of his clever tack-down-tide manoeuvre. The sudden appearance dead ahead of the Class III walking wounded dries up his smile like a match-box joke. It only needs our wet friend up forward to begin shrieking sail numbers in a voice broken with triumph for the owner to go into his special kiss-me-Hardy act. Receiving no confirmation of his discovery from the nest, our lad breaks parole and comes trotting aft for his pat and biscuit. The private patient by-passing a surgery full of N.H.S. veterans will meet a friendlier battery of eyes.

Not every owner will lend his bottles as freely of course. The binoculars on some ships, be it inscribed field glasses with which the object has to be pursued like the pea and thimble game or an amazing-offer-cannot-be-repeated instrument which incorporates half a tank turret is just another of those symbols of ownership.

The master will watch a stranger's fingers close around them in the half-certainty that the man will at once produce Dan Leno boots and go scampering around the decks juggling with the instrument. It takes more than the white gleam of knuckles and a strap round the neck to reassure him. I have seen an owner watching Blanche's boy ('Oh I wish I had a camera...') toddle around the deck with the binoculars swinging wildly from his tiny bull neck like Gog laying waste with his club. It is hard to repress a grin — the foam-flecked jaw and fingers snapping rapidly open and shut as if he was playing an invisible pin-ball bagatelle game give further proof of the owner's scarce-repressed mirth.

Old Harry, wearing on his chest a pair of monstrous brass field glasses like a Guard Room fire alarm, has no such hesitation about lending them.

'Here, try these,' he'll challenge, clapping them to your brow with stunning force. The stranger, peering into those murky caverns will recoil with a cry of horror and disgust as he stares in fascination at what appears to be a host of tarantulas advancing in a snowstorm along the coach roof. But, as Harry says, skilfully thrusting thumb into sweater sleeve to polish the delicate bloom of the object lenses...

'Money wouldn't buy a glass like that in the market today.'

Old Harry's Bunkside Book

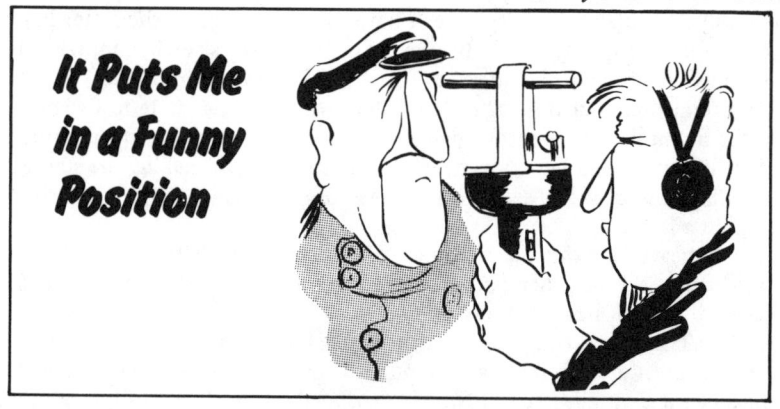

It Puts Me in a Funny Position

THE NAVIGATOR WHO cultivates the trick, twice a watch, of asking 'Who's on the helm?' in a chilly tone (while thoughtfully tapping his teeth with a pencil) ensures himself against personal blame later when the ship has settled gratefully upon her ear in haunts of red-shank and bait-digger.

The tidal atlas – the navigator's friend – is the biggest alibi of the lot. He works through his twelve little pictures, ends up where he started and finds that he has lost an hour on the way. Our mathematician can work out his lies to the last decimal place while being swept magnificently broadside up-Channel like an old lady athwart the commuters with her platform ticket, out to meet father on the four-thirty and destined to fetch up in Esher.

'Actually,' says our friend later, rubbing out frantically, 'we must be prepared to have been set a little to the east'ard.'

Science has not robbed this ancient art of its charm though. Radio aids have brought accuracy within the reach of all. A familiar sight to all who have lain wakeful on the weather settee berth is the navigator with his Heron lurching around the saloon looking for a null, his great head wagging to and fro like a dog with a bone. I have seen men ransack the ship in search of a null rolling their eyes pitiably while the ship's company wait silently. That atmosphere of hushed suffering broken only by the dragging shuffle of feet is like midnight in the Jermyn Street Turkish Bath.

Radio direction finding is a simple matter. Memorising in advance three selected call signs, our man waits with an easy smile on his face until the beeps begin then swings into smooth action.

'Da, da diddy da,' he mutters insanely thrusting his ferrite rod into the shrinking face of the man on the settee berth.

'Dit dit dah dit dah!' he foams, swinging suddenly to confront the cook.

He wanders off into an open oilskin locker still giving his poor mad cry and some merciful fellow slams the door on him.

Strength of mind is called for in working a D.F. position. The less self-disciplined, unable to wait for their station signals to come up, find louder and better signals hemming them in on all sides and forgetting their original choice, go shopping around from one to another, jotting down morse

Old Harry's Bunkside Book

on any flat, blank, matt surface. I have heard the man in the settee berth screaming for quarter while the navigator tattooed his cerebellum with the Outer Gabbard and all stations to Ushant right down to his dorsal.

I remember a distressing little incident when Old Harry, in festive mood after a wheel trick spent exchanging friendly banter with a fleet of drift-net fishermen who lay athwart his course, came below making the staccato droning sound which satisfies his urge to song. The navigator swung on him in a flash.

'By heaven it's the Muckle Flugga,' he barked, searching for a null.

Only a skilfully handled bucket, temporarily imprisoning our hero, saved that navigator from mischief.

Old Harry, who normally distrusts any wireless set which lacks a walnut cabinet and a bubbling accumulator, was once persuaded to don the head-set and try his fist at a D.F. fix. Gripped by the drama of his task and adopting the easy crouch of the Cornish wrestler he began bounding around the saloon tethered by his flex and roaring stern injunctions to stand clear. He finally cornered Start Point in the owner's locker and triumphantly whipped open the door to reveal a private store of honey.

Mainstay of every navigator is still the carefully entered log-book. The man whose chart-work shows tight little cocked hats instead of the vast solar topees common to the rest of us will know the value of a log entered in a neat, crimped handwriting suggestive of infinite precision. In the family cruiser, however, these entries may often lack accuracy.

Starting with a page-heading in bold and confident hand plus carefully copied tidal data, high water Dover and firmly ruled lines in anticipation of the longest passage since De Lesseps dug his way out of Egypt, the entries record departure and the streaming of the log. They continue as the miles reel astern, gay with little references to what Norma said about the potted meat and gradually settling down to a more economical style.

The watch changes and we find entries apparently made with the thick end of a fid and suggested a worsening of the weather — a massive unical script reads:

'18.00 hrs. — lob 50 — wink F9 — changed jeb, reefed mam.'

A half-pint of salt water and the imprint of cocoa spoon completes the entry. The brevity of succeeding entries hints at a night of sore trial. A raisin marking Reed's at the page dealing with single-letter signals and a pair of wet trousers marking the spot usually occupied by the navigator tells its own grim tale. The log will always peter out after the first landfall leaving an unchronicled tale of alarms and triumphs which the abrupt and final entry 'Anchored 5 Ftm.' made in a firm and well nourished hand two days after arrival does nothing to improve.

Harry, who uses his charts as log-books and to whom variation is a dirty word, sets great pride by these tattered publications. Handed down from father to son he has amended his own charts from personal observations, a method which suggests that the entire sea-bed is in a state of constant upheaval, shoving out banks and rocks and whipping them back again smartly like Galley Alley demonstrators. The present buoyage system, which does not figure on Harry's charts, is the subject of a great deal of violent wrath and the watch on many a light-ship has stood rooted with alarm as the light beam picks out that accusing figure.

Until recently he relied for verification of position upon the noisome samples brought up on his lead-arming. He learned many a trick from fishermen in his youth and not least the importance of the tooth and the palate in distinguishing Kentish rag from *bl.gy.m. and f.s.* There was a regrettable incident when he sampled the bottom astern of a P.L.A. hopper and confirmed a position which would have required the sanction of the Public Health Authorities.

Nowadays, armed with an ex-aircraft landing compass which came into his possession wrapped in a sock and equivalent to an impressive rank of Bass bottles, he is able to plot massive fixes which look like badly built rook's nests. Lacking a torch in the handle, however, this instrument used at night requires him to hold above his head a flaming cresset — a commanding spectacle and one which is giving local folk lore a new and unearthly chapter.

Seamanship

NOBODY EVER SEES it when it's good but just get a line around your ensign staff when leaving the berth and every door and window for miles around is black with bodies. It is the greatest source of blind panic. Let father explain the forthcoming manoeuvre how he will, station his fender-danglers and issue his orders in a low and beautifully enunciated voice, it will only be a matter of time before he is rolling his eyes like a clockwork cobbler.

It's All Right Once You're In

THERE'S A SHARP divergence of interests between those who go *in* the water and those who go *on* it. Your yachtsman, his face framed in personal buoyancy like a plum on a tinned peach, glares his hostility at the swimmers athwart his course. They thresh clear of his foaming forefoot with sharp cries of impracticable advice and suggestion.

'I just don't know what we're coming to these days!' he laments holding a steady course for the sewer outfall.

A dog can be ejected from armchair into the rainy night with more eager anticipation than the traditional yachtsman makes an invigorating plunge from cockpit. On rare occasions and in gala mood and sizzling heat when even his linen hat and navy knickers have failed to work their cooling magic, he may consent to be towed astern on a bowline or even to breast-stroke his way majestically around the topsides commenting on the quality of antifouling. He will still be hauled out mottled like a political map with his convictions unshaken as he hastens below to shake them over the saloon settees.

For men of lesser stature the first swim of the season, outcome of sudden and reckless decision, becomes a humourless affair from the moment that trousers hit the cabin sole. The sun goes behind a cloud with uncanny haste. Emerging on deck towering whitely upon cringing feet and feeling as vulnerable as a hermit crab out of its shell he holds out a ribbed chest like a canteen of cutlery and stands around with arms folded discussing the rigging.

There is a built-in vindictiveness about the man who goes in first. Shrivelled to temporary inarticulation by the sudden deadly chill he rises to the surface on drumming feet. 'Ahhh, that's better,' he howls in a voice like a ventriloquist's doll, 'come on in it's lovely!'

Among offshore racing men, the flat and hopeless calm which drives the owners to crawl round on hands and knees issuing waspish rebukes to those who move in jerks, sees expectancy dawn on less dedicated faces. The accumulated layers of clothing, which like the yearly rings of the oak, keep tally on the length of the passage are removed with lessening caution and the first smears of Nivea cream appear on the chart table.

'I see they're swimming on "Whirligig",' mourns a small voice. The owner gives his benediction with the defeated air of a man who has drained the bitter wine of defeat and is starting work on the cork.

There is a rough male tradition that one should swim in the stark on these occasions. A false and gusty humour prevails as man after man emerges at the double from below, either juggling with a towel or bounding for the rail with averted eyes. Percy, gazing his own height, toes a runner wire at speed and cleaves the water with a haunting cackle of a marsh fowl.

The monstrous effort of hauling one'self back aboard unaided is another convention. 'Oh I can manage thanks!' flute our athletes. The ship shudders like a washing machine on the final spin as each man, biceps vibrating and eyes bulging, collapses through the rail to lie making a plucky attempt at conversation with what remains of his wind.

The family cruiser on the other hand is haunted by the demands of the swimmer.

'Daddy will find us a nice little beach' is a cry which involves our master in navigational nightmares aimed at quelling rebellion. The best beaches involve an anchorage off which is about as secure as antlers hung on Scotch tape and include a landing through heavy surf. The strip of white beach viewed through binoculars from a more practical berth resolves itself into a ridge of broken shell that would cripple a rhino, fronting a mudhole already tenanted by a pair of bicycle handlebars and a submerged sack eloquent with gloomy possibilities. Eventually the party rows ashore to some crab-haunted salting where father's efforts to rally the picnic spirit ('Who'd like a ride on daddy's back?') are noted with unsympathetic scorn like the late-arrivals indicator on Paddington Station.

Old Harry, who has never held with swimming, has always nursed the conviction that it would come naturally to him if the need arose. He demonstrated this truth with startling effect the time he went out on his crosstrees to see where they'd put the Nab Tower. The collapse of this strut under its intolerable burden launched him into space where he was briefly visible in silhouette galloping on air, his smock ballooning, like some husky oilskin ballerina late for her cue.

The water which erupted on his entry was still raining down as he came up and reputable observers insist that he ran along the surface and straight up the topsides. He was halfway up the forestay before merciful hands could drag him down.

I Heard a Little Hiss

THOSE ADVERTISEMENTS WHICH show a bikini-clad dolly pumping up her inflatable boat and nearly dying of laughter in the process are not always a strictly accurate representation of fact. Given a worn-out foot bellows, a kinked pipe and a faulty valve the laughter which this exercise generates rates for sheer howling fun with a wet station year and a flat battery at 2 a.m.

The learner-driver braking benevolently and abruptly at every pedestrian crossing tires of this gracious novelty at about the same rate as children exhaust the novelty of pumping up daddy's boat. The chore, earmarked at once for mother, sees more than one domestic crisis precipitated. With the bag inflating under her listless toe at about the same speed as a souffle in a chilly oven, the master is unable to contain his impatience.

'It should take four minutes' he rasps, 'Oh come here let *me* do it!'

He opens up with a spirited tarantella for one toe which serves the dual purposes of rebuke and rapid inflation. Within two minutes he is down to a laboured limp and the generous gustiness of his tortured breathing contrasts sharply with the peevish whistle of air in the valve.

The new owner is slow to believe makers' claims (justifiable) that 'puncturing is highly unlikely.' He treats his passengers with a black suspicion that implies that each is equipped with more spikes than a wardog and scheming privately to get at the valves. A nervous habit of frisking them persists.

'I hate to imagine what poor Enid thought!' comments the wife with crisp displeasure. 'It was less the way you pulled her ankles up to look at her heels than your thoughtless remark about wanting to see what she'd got on!'

Neither do new owners accept readily the assurances that it is safe to stand on the bottom. Wading around in yielding neoprene billows like some outlandish insect in the picnic jam, and with scalp shuttling back and forth in doubt, it takes just one humorist ashore to whistle sharply through his teeth and our man is out of it and yelling for his air-bottle.

What to do with it at sea is a recurring problem. Reluctant to release air which has been won so hardily they lack room on deck for stowage.

'There's no reason why we shouldn't tow it, it's a quiet day' reasons father, stepping into the world of prophecy.

Old Harry's Bunkside Book

Later, concentrating on luff, compass, echo-sounder and the encouraging but fictional excesses of the speed-meter he is deaf to the entreaties of a crew who are watching the eagle's flight of the boat astern. Father, happily demonstrating how he won the unrated cruiser race has bare time to comment.

'We'll soon be under the lee' when the dinghy rises from the water and claps down over the cockpit like the lid of a biscuit barrel.

When it comes to fighting off an attack by a rubber boat a man needs a shotgun. The wisp of tissue paper ritually slapped around a loaf of bread is about as empty a gesture to the demands of hygiene as your helmsman laying about him with the tiller.

The satisfaction of being able to crash alongside with indifference for topside paint is also hard to accept and for those who aim to lie alongside Old Harry, apt to be short-lived. With a steel fid stuck out through a water outlet in the temporary absence of the fitting (a matter of a visit to the plumber's junk heap for an old bath plug of the correct diameter), the visitor's cheery hail is drowned in the 'fffroof' of escaping air, followed at once by the twin slaps of fingers finding the rail. Whitening knuckles provide the sole evidence of a guest's safe arrival.

Old Harry, who saw service (through field glasses) in India, brought back many souvenirs of those sun-drenched years. Apart from the group photo of mustachioed men squatting with folded arms as if expressing adamant disassociation from the slain and diminutive tiger at their feet, there is also the elephant's foot umbrella stand. This novelty, placed in the porch, sees many an unwary nocturnal visitor go thudding backwards down the area steps, shod improbably and goaded by a shooting stick up the hacking vent.

Not least of these foreign curios is his mussuck. Having noted how the simple peasants could propel themselves across the Ganges on a goat-skin, inflated via one leg. Old Harry swiftly adapted the method to his own needs. A visit to the knacker's yard having provided two mussucks at trifling cost it remained only to inflate them (a nostalgic sight for exiled Highlanders) and last an old pipecot across the top to provide an inflatable boat at a sensible price complete with eight masts and a terrifying smell.

Paddling rapidly to windward of the club on his maiden trip, his heart warmed to the cries of surprise and admiration for his originality. Nodding agreeably to the Commodore's lady, he failed to take offence at her gasps of disgust as she pressed dainty handkerchief to nostril.

'Nothing here that a bit of salt won't cure' he assured her, slapping his hairy vessel. Simultaneously a volley of eight corks shot skywards and our friend was seen briefly paddling in a blur of action for the shore to an arpeggio of raspberry accompaniment from the legs before the waters claimed their prize.

Old Harry's Bunkside Book

Comic Turn

THE DEVELOPMENT OF the small modern yacht with ever-shrinking deck space has shaken yachtsmen down into their cockpits like beans in a plug-hole. The winch has taken the place of the tackle, and where once the air rang to the bubbling scream of the mate with his quiff jammed in the jib purchase, we now have the ring of winches and the metallic chatter as Percy, goaded by the owner's clear soprano, endeavours to fit handle into socket.

This improvement carries a penalty. Every owner lives in dread of losing his handles and nurses a suspicion that once his back is turned the crew go skipping round the deck lobbing handles overboard like peasants sowing spring oats. Even those ratchet handles which suddenly slip and launch the operator outboard with the acceleration of cinema audiences trying to beat the anthem to the exit do no more than bring a twisted smile to his worried features.

Sheet winches hold many a terror for the tyro. The riding turn is discovered by him in triumph but his laughing cry of 'Look fellers, No hands!' dies away like a church organ in a power cut as his gaze travels the circle of hardening jaws around him.

To make best use of the pudding-mixing technique of the family crew, the little force must be deployed with care. We'll have Percy on the lee job sheet all ready to cast off the turns of the main sheet in error, uncle (crepe soles) ready to wind in three fathoms of slack before he gets to the meat and Blanche's boy on the runners prepared to snap them down on any available boot.

'Here we go then' laughs the owner in his innocence.

Spinnaker work sees the whole crowd working away like mechanical drummers on a steam organ while two figures up forward pedal air in their efforts to retrieve a pole which is hooked to both clews and nothing else. Later, marbles sorted and Percy on the guy winch, the mate on the foredeck beckons a finger.

'Give me an inch of pole' he drawls.

He gets twelve feet of it and a new hair style as it whistles over his crust en route for the forestay where it points sternly at the fleet ahead like Kitchener wanting somebody.

Old Harry's Bunkside Book

The cockpit team of a real racer follows sterner technique. Owners recognise their men only by their quivering trousers. The aim is to home the sheet without having to apply more than two clicks with the handle and a keen racing crew should fight to get at the winch day or night. A case in point is the man who quits his bunk to sneak up on deck and relieve his doubt about the weather. Note his appreciative chuckle when he finds that he is just in nice time to help put the ship about. With shirt-tails flogging in the clean no'easterly and socks lapping up cockpit drainage like thirsty puppies he is a credit to the game. Later, creeping below spouting water with hair plastered round his forehead like a generous helping of gravy on a meagre dumpling we still hear his mutter of approbation as he climbs back into the sack.

The two-man night watch ('You take Sidney but don't let him steer') sees ample opportunity for the newcomer to master the winches. Our tyro settles on the floor of the cockpit, gazing at the stars which swoop between his shivering kneecaps and debates the merits of sticking his head down the hatch for the warm updraft and stomaching the heady overtones of wet wool, pipe smoke and burnt bacon. The mate, who has lost a steady half-know since he took over, begins the business.

'I wonder if you can see my luff' he inquires coyly. Our friend struggles up and casts it an unloving and uncomprehending glance.

'we might ease it a cat's whisker' muses the helmsman.

Our tyro lifts off the turns with stealthy caution as if easing up lino in search of beetles. He surges six foot of sheet with a bang that brings up the crew like High School fire-drill.

Old Harry (who thinks that 'mechanical advantage' is what's taken of him everytime he pays his garage bill and that 'a ratio' commanded H.M.S. 'Victory' at Trafalgar) has been tardy in blessing the sheet winch with his approval. Accustomed to great bights of swollen sisal which have to be stuffed through fairleads with wary concentration like feeding a parrot, his first encounter with winches was not without drama. Taking a swift turn he mustered all hands and using the handle as an incentive to their efforts, had them whip in the sheet at the run, a method which brought a tortured shriek from the bearings and a jet of steam from the oil hole.

Once the true purpose of the handles was explained he became a man to reckon with. Any owner with such little foibles as wearing their club ties at sea do well to stand back. With such a little foible trapped by Harry's lightning turns, only the quick-witted use of scissors can win him freedom.

Who Said 'Let Go'?

THE ART AND science of anchoring evokes more emotion than a trainee bailiff or the Sale of Old Dobbin. 'I'm sorry but I won't be spoken to like that!' shrills the owner's wife up forward and ordered to let go. The owner in fascinated stupor and bereft of further speech eyes the narrowing gap between bow and seawall. They hit it with a crash like an acrobat in a timpano.

You'll see brave men, veterans of many a crisis, approach an anchorage munching their 10in cigars like a hamster with a string bean. What chance has your nervous tyro, circling the anchorage like a questing honey bee? He has his dainty included-in-standard-inventory anchor, still with its label on, and the basic 15 fathoms of underweight chain as dished out by the builder with the paucity of a baker putting jam in a doughnut. He finds an unsuitable site. 'Let go' he pipes. Counsin Stanley lobs the pretty thing overboard. 'All gone' he advises with stark albeit unwitting truth as the last link of the bitter end flicks out of the chain pipe.

Your inexperienced owner, anchoring for the first time, goes ashore reluctantly and heavy with foreboding. Walking backwards and staring with a glassy fixity that would make Lot's Wife look like a minor Deacon in a lingerie department, he is coaxed into a restaurant. Sitting there, listening for a rising wind, the expresso machine triggers him up on his feet with the speed of an opposition back bencher spotting an injustice. He settles back with knife and fork and gloomily quarters his club tie which has draped itself across his *haricot vert*.

He is also alert to official requirements and harbour bylaws. He goes ashore determined to pay money to somebody. He approaches the first peaked cap he sees, which happens to be worn by a convalescing gas inspector from Woking.

'Excuse me' he says, enunciating in the special voice he saves for doctors and parsons, 'I spent the night between *Liz O' Lymington* and *Polly of Poole* but would you prefer me on the trot? I've got a little yellow Barbel' he adds, clarifying the matter. 'It don't matter what colour it is, mate,' the gas inspector tells him, 'trottin' gallopin' or riding a bike.'

Old Harry's Bunkside Book

The technical phraseology of anchoring can confuse not only the beginner but also the foreigner. The latter, in a regrettable shirt, is welcomed to Merry England by the Harbour Master ('Yew can't lie there sor'.) with a warmth that has brought old traitor tear to many a manly eye. Thereafter, and eyed by those already anchored with the grudging acceptance of railway commuters for the late shopper, the dialogue becomes confusing.

'Are you thinking of bringing up?' queries one. 'You've got a soft bottom there,' remarks another. 'Don't lie here, I've just fouled my bower,' cautions a third helpfully. Our worried tyro is no better off. Having performed his evolutions under the appreciative eyes of forty people eating tea, and having concluded the screaming repartee with his wife, he brings up. She at once goes below not wishing to make a further 'ridiculous exhibition of herself' A man in shorts with a pale abdomen like a stack of rolled diplomas comes to the bow of his craft and stares long and pointedly at the modest gap between the craft. 'Is she lying back?' he asks, talking through his nose. 'Oh yes,' says our tyro, 'and she's got her shoes off too'.

The sight of mum in the bow, bending to her task, headscarf and red stretch pants like a London bus backing out of the depot, is a familiar one to the cruiser owner. Equally familiar when about to anchor is the effect that the command to let go seems to have on any foredeck party. Moving with dream-like slowness in an *adagio* superbly economical of effort, the foredeck party gingers the owner at his useless heim into his *entrechat* like a stung whippet. 'Let it out, LET IT OUT' he weeps executing a *tour en aire* and stunning himself on the boom. On short scope the anchor is holding like a snake in a bag of marbles. Percy glides aft. 'I'm sorry, I didn't quite catch that', he apologises warmly. The owner unships the tiller.

The little rituals of the anchorage, like the silent communion of men along the rail after returning aboard at night, are not to be ignored. Take the owner's first enchanted survey of his estate upon rising prior to an early start. The morn trembles with the promise of a hot day and the gossamer mists swirl above the drying mud banks. He gazes contented at the glistening wet mud, noting with amused sympathy somebody's anchor left high and dry. 'Why some poor fool has got his an . . .' be begins, smile slowly withering as his eye follows the cable. Happy are they who sail sandy waters and know no mud.

Raising anchor in Gashouse Creek is an experience to daunt a hippo. A noxious burping of oily bubbles heralds the appearance of the anchor with its slobbery bonus of ooze and the regulation bicycle tyre slung over the fluke. No new intake student nurse doing her first stint at the sluices handles her task with less love than mum decking her anchor. With plastic bucket she prepares to wash down. Father, seated on the sidedeck to watch the genoa is in fine fettle after a secure night's anchorage. 'Well you know what you've got with a muddy bottom' he explains, as a wave of slime washes aft.

Unlike your ocean racing yachtsman to whom the order to unearth the

Old Harry's Bunkside Book

best bower from below the cabin sole seems as incongruous as asking a Knight of the Bedchamber for a potty, Old Harry is a master of the art and he welcomes any chance of exhibiting his skills. His 'running moor' is a firm favourite. His best bower is about the weight of an emigrant's suitcase, handy on deck as horserake and it holds like a church pew splinter in a knitted jumper suit. The splash when it is let go has been known to swamp a chain ferry and on one occasion ten old men in esplanade wheel chairs got their ball races soaked.

Letting out cable which once kept dogs off a municipal floral clock he comes thundering in under a cloud of rust, dust, spiders and long lost trouser buttons and brings up with a slam that dislodges the bogey stove and unships his spotted dick. He places his kedge, middles on both and then leaning on his rail, looks around at his audience ripe for genial conversation. He hails a nearby wife who has just come up on deck to cool her trifle. 'Madam, tell your husband to keckle his warp before he gets into trouble with his hawse', he advises kindly. Stunned, she hurries below dropping her petit fours as she goes.

Ordinarily, he allows himself a swinging circle like an Olympic stadium and which nobody contests. In a blow his vessel offers more windage than a confessional on the Cresta run which combined with drawing more water than a Liffey brewery makes for a behaviour at anchor as unpredictable as a Bank Holiday milk delivery. More cetain is the behaviour of all other vessels at anchor nearby when Old Harry gets under way. As his cable begins to come aboard the entire fleet silently glides towards him until he is ringed by early morning faces demanding justice. An old gentleman in Household Cavalry pyjamas appears in his hatch smacking his gums. 'I ffray ffir, itff juft not good enough. Youff fouled our anchorff!' he complains. Gathering together the assortment of ground tackle as it comes dripping into view, Old Harry, now making good way, and with seamanlike concern, tows them well clear of the dangerous harbour entrance before letting them go.

Marina Amenities

DEVELOPERS, WHO BELIEVE that Constable Country is some kind of police radar trap and consider any heath or dell the better for a quick skim of cement, unerringly select either bird sanctuary or quiet creek for marina

Old Harry's Bunkside Book

development — the better if the creek has been tenanted by private flywheel and gas cooker moorings since dot. It is a sad fact that if wild ducks are considered socially acceptable and A Good Thing, yachts and yachtsmen, being A Healthy Thing, are even better. The more so since ducks don't buy chalets.

When Old Harry was told that theodolites had been spotted in Gas House Creek he expressed the hope that they would breed and the opinion that they must be there for the sprats. Later, assuming that these instruments on their tripods were an early stage in the production of picture postcards, he obliged by posing in that frozen, backwards-falling attitude peculiar to the foreground of vintage sepia tramcar and seafront views. Upon learning the terrible truth, however, he rallied his friends from their bollards on the quay. Working at speed they gathered and transferred the high tide mark of squeezy bottles, left foot flip-flops and nasty foreign medicine bottles to a level which, had it been fact, would have inundated Harrods. The developers turned their attentions to Iona.

Marinas vary from a hole in the mud, a poles and string affair, to the French Fishing Village facsmile, all period pantile and a transistorised wailing widow on every plot where you can slam yourself silly on simulated low beams for £5,000 a go. Some are real harbours lightly fringed by amenities while others are real amenities lightly fringed by harbour where you can plug in or hook up to every civilised delight from Dial-a-Prayer to the latest Watergate. I have seen yachts so trussed and girded by pipes and power cables that they looked like a shop window display of foundation garments for matrons. There was an owner who got under way, forgetting to unplug. His wife shot out through the after hatch on the power line, wearing hair drier and girdle and he made it as far as the hailing station with the water hose stretched astern and humming like the Orpheus Choir. 'Just testing engines, I'll be coming straight back,' he prophesied to the goggling Berthing Master, whereupon the hose took over and whipped him back into his berth butt first and howling with the speed of a striking cobra. His stern hit the catwalk and projected a marina trolley into the unsuspecting tail of Lady Blanchbrisket who rode it screaming into berth P14.

Amenities vary too. They range from one dribbling shower, a windowsill full of rusting razor blades and more writing on the wall than Tutankhamun's Tomb, to the mosaic and Old Spice temples of toiletry with hot air hand driers where you stand like Uncle Tom waiting for his manacles. There are marinas where you stand midway on springing gangplanks with your cardboard box of provisions, bounding higher and ever higher until the molluscs claim you for their own and there are others where you have to put your son's name down for a berth at baptism. One false move and you are out. You flash a letterbox grin at the Manager and tuck the St Michael's tab on your vest out of sight as he passes. I have seen grown men, accused of shopping at Super Save, conducted sobbing from their berths. Many applicants for berths are refused upon blurting the fact that they intend to go sailing *every* weekend and slink away with sad demenure ('Demenure turning me down, Sir?').

Old Harry's Bunkside Book

It seems to be established that 60 per cent of berth holders prefer to stay inside at weekends. The lofty wheelhouses of these all-top-and-transom pagodas give their owners a decided superiority over owners at lower level, witness the arrival of one such owner at a berth occupied by Old Harry's converted scallop-drubbler. 'Ahoy,' he blasted, at close range through his Tannoy, 'are you likely to be long in that berth, skipper?' Old Harry looked long and thoughtfully at the cast, spluttering edifice nearby. 'If you put that box of bricks alongside 'o me I'll be not only long but thin and narrer as well,' he summed up.

A deepening embarrassment in marinas is the use of the ship's toilet. 'We prefer owners to make full use of facilities provided,' the Management says, choosing its words with care. What they get is a morning cacophony from 500 transistor radios with as many owners artfully pumping out in time to the music. There is the added problem of the boat with the self-contained chemical can and the owner, lumbered with a sealed bag of effluent tip-toeing ashore after dark. 'Right sir,' rasps HM Customs officer stepping out of concealment, 'What's in that bag eh?' The owner tells him. In a word. 'Very comical sir,' grits the office, 'I think I'll take charge of that.' The scene winds to its nasty denouement. In the smaller cruisers where use of the heads calls for a certain amount of athleticism, an owner and his crew are at some disadvantage. They wait until there are no toe-caps visible on the catwalk and with mission accomplished rise with casual dignity from the forehatch to hoist their pants. The owner of one small gaff cutter had reached this stage. Whistling thinly to divert attention from his busy fumbling he became the target for Old Harry who was studying the man's rigging. 'I see you've been keckling your cranse,' he noted approvingly. The man shot back into his cuddy like some polyp alert to predatory foe.

The approach and berthing manoeuvres made necessary by marina use produces exhibitions of seamanship unequalled since Noah hit Arrarat. If on the helm of another man's boat when the final approach draws near one should vacate it with a laughing compliment to the host's superior skill otherwise he will be at your elbow grunting and hissing like a vacuum pump. 'Usually I come in just the *teeniest* bit slower', he sobs, eyeing the tumbling bow-wave. The master of marina diplomacy has a different tactic. 'Why,' he laughs, clapping you on the back, 'you're a man after my own heart. I'll bet you take a wide swing, cut to half throttle at that post and then, when your bow is abeam of the pontoon, you'll come full astern.' Old Harry, that master of the Gravesend luff and the running moor, never fails to put on a show that rivets his audience. Berthing Masters have needed surgery just to get their fingers unclasped and one required a tracheotomy to recover his cap badge, another took holy orders and a third was last seen playing violin outside Harringay.

In he comes all bellow, bucket and bowsprit, weaving through the weekend Westerlies, Ghengis Khan in a girl's school, topside thundering, knifing bobstay and butt joints a'grind like a waste disposal unit gagging on hotel toast. He luffs for a vacant berth. A marina boatman is performing a series of gigantic leaps while waving both hands above his head.

Old Harry's Bunkside Book

'Don't worry,' hails Old Harry, 'I'll carry my way.' Not only does he carry his way but a large section of pontoon, including the boatman, with it. Punted out into the spring ebb this honest fellow is last seen passing the Nab and making good time. Old Harry brings up with his bowsprit impaling the window of the men's showers, where it turns the regulator to *hot*. Two pink piggy-bank military gentlemen emerge roaring and steaming like the old Royal Scot leaving York.

Don't Just Stand There

THOSE OF US who plough the lonely furrow over bank and spit rejoice at the evolution of the twin-keeler. Dotted around the drying sands of inlet and estuary and rendered monumental by distance you'll see them etched against the Sunday sunset.

Not for these owners though are the artifices of sugging, heeling down and kedge-work. Their crews are spared the O'Grady Says charade of all-up-in-th-bow and all-jump-together (a sobering little exercise if ever there was one) and assuming they went on bolt upright and on a fast ebb they are as timelessly wedded to earth as the Admiralty Arch — pending the next flood. Unlike the *Swan Lake* death scene of the keeled yacht, settling on her ear to an accompaniment of elephantine internal rumblings while her crew on nimble toe mount the heeling decks, our twin, upright as a boys' club treasurer, offers a frontier watch tower from which to note the changing scene.

A strange rapport exists between the newly grounded twin and passing yachtsmen in conventional craft. 'They're on all right,' these exchange with fierce interest. To offer succour would be as pointless as handing leaflets to a man with both feet stuck in a drain; to speak would imply a sense of superiority. With the twin dried out on her bank, standing straddled like an old man looking down a coalhole, passing yachtsmen tap their noses, size up the case as hopeless and gaze glassily ahead as if avoiding one of those prophets in sandshoes who lay in wait outside tube stations with six boxes of matches, a mutter and a mad glint.

Not that drying out in a twin is free of all complication. There is the bait-digger whose tireless sapping around each keel, like the patient bumbling of the dung beetle, is rewarded by a spectacle out of all proportion to his efforts. There is also the fore-and-aft trim of the smaller twin-keel

Old Harry's Bunkside Book

cruiser to consider. While Blanche is straining her blue serge to the limit in her efforts to lug a mattress up through the forehatch it only needs a sudden concentration of male might in the cockpit to unsettle the seesaw. 'Let's have a look at that bubble in her gel-coat' invites Father striding aft and launching his spouse over the pulpit.

Neither do keels in pairs always make for smooth seamanship. Take letting go the mooring. 'ALL GONE' cries the foredecksman triumphantly and mistakenly. The ship bounds forward only to bring up short with a vicious curtsey as the buoyrope hooks a keel. The helmsman, who is regarding his tiller as if it had turned into a snake, feels the wind of the scything boom pass his ear and lets loose a falsetto string of contradictory orders which if obeyed to the letter would have the foredeck quartet form a human pyramid, top man juggling with winch handles. He peers over the side, thirsty for knowledge, loses his cap and as an encore launches himself off in pursuit in a dinghy without oars.

The prospective buyer mulling over a heap of brochures is tossed on a sea of doubts between aerodynamically designed keels guaranteed to lift him to windward, like the time Old Harry caught his braces in the haybaler, and boats with the sort of headroom that calls for a paper hanger's trestle when he wants to sponge his Vynide. His finger traces line by line down magazine write-ups in search of veiled message or hidden implication and he takes his trial sail with the mounting uncertainty of a novicate on the eve of her vows '. . . and when you want to sponge your Vynide, sir . . .' continues the salesman, midway through his harangue and with one knee surreptitiously pressed against the tiller to reduce weather helm. He takes time off to demonstrate a tip-up table about as ill-conceived as the glass shelf above a washbasin — which rewards the stooping ablutionist either with a crack on the occipital or a water tap up each nostril.

With her dark secrets out of sight a twin-keeler of substantial size peacefully at anchor in 2ft of water attracts newcomers with conventional draught like a goat staked out for the marauding tiger. 'What have you got, sir?' hail these owners standing resolutely inshore. 'Come aboard and I'll show you my standard equipment' pipes the proud neophyte from his firm and motionless platform, misinterpreting this anxious query. The visiting yacht judders to a standstill, her crew crying 'WE'RE ON' in Greek chorus and taking two smart paces forward as if on pay parade. The tyro up in the bows lets go his anchor on reflex and looks aft for congratulation.

Whatever the disadvantages of returning to the shore at midnight with water-carriers, two sliced loaves and a veal and egg pie to find his biped separated by 60 yards of hissing, popping ooze the twin-keeler man is at least spared the *danse macabre* of a turning tide, a foul berth and pyjama-clad figures juggling kedges. The rightful tenant of the anchorage and earliest arrival, face framed in his porthole, watches with about as much warmth of expression as a Moray eel in an amphora. He is doomed to a night of thuds and apologies. The flanking boats are pushed apart again and their owners stand meditating on the insubstantial gap. 'Ektually,' they honk 'we should lie clear of your now.' A fitful breeze flutters the nightwear and the yachts fly together again like long parted lovers.

Old Harry's Bunkside Book

Dried out, the twin-keeler may look like the rear end of a lady golfer faced with a difficult putt but afloat you'd never know how many keels she'd got. Heeled to a breeze with one leg out of water she (the yacht) only needs leotards and a pianist in a knitted cardigan to look like a primary grade ballerina doing a work-out for Southend Drama Week. 'When you were lying over yesterday *I could see your little skeg*' confides one owner to another in the cathedral hush of the railway carriage next day.

Old Harry, who once dried out standing bolt upright on his ballast keel and spent the next 6 hours sitting dead amidships vertically erect with a cornish pasty between his front teeth frightened to chew, withholds judgement on twin-keelers. Aware of the unique advantages they offer for his particular style of pilotage he views the appearance of a windward keel above water with the jocular fascination once reserved for the buttoned boot.

Finance and Figures

MASTERY OF THE twelve times multiplication table was the crowning peak of my scholastic achievement, chanted triumphantly in the company of a score of other jug-eared nippers. The arrival of metrication is a blow which has brought me to my knees. I try to *think* metric. The notion that kilos and anchors can have anything in common is as incongruous as a nun in bicycle clips.

Immaculate Condition

AN OWNER WITH his boat up for sale seems to fluctuate between apologetic extortion and uneasy guilt.

'End of season snip' proclaims his advertisement, 'immaculate condition, lavishly fitted out, must sell . . .' He reads his little composition in print with sinking heart. He is leadenly aware of his boat for the first time from an outsider's viewpoint. She's as immaculate as a roller-towel in a machine-shop ablutions.

'I think I'll try to brighten her up a bit' he falters, panicking at the thought of a thundering horde of purchasers. He lays about him with the old self-adhesive plastic, adding wrinkled tiles to the galley with easy disregard for irregularities of planking and slapping up marble-pattern in the heads. It takes on the Spartan chilliness of a family mausoleum. All it lacks is a flight of bats.

His first enquirer arrives simultaneously with his first mouthful of supper, necessitating a dragging approach to the front door with jaws champing at a dizzy speed. Behind him the oven clangs on his plate promising a shrunken chop and rattling peas.

Decision on asking price imposes severe strain on the sensitive man. Like a road-worker repairing a traffic bollard he sticks it up fifty pounds in the pessimistic certainty that it'll be knocked down again.

'Actually, I was thinking of asking six-and-a-half', he laughs toothily, reluctant to mention money in more specific terms. The buyer, who knows his job, allows a long and terrible silence to develop.

'Of course I've done a lot to her . . .' our friend croaks. He winces at a

Old Harry's Bunkside Book

mental flash-back featuring a gaping butt and caulking fed in until it comes writhing out of the forehatch. The silence grows. 'That includes the dinghy . . .' he tells the mantelpiece . . . 'and the outboard', he grates, minutes later.

Equally exacting is the realisation that he has asked too little. The fact is betrayed either by a cheque slapped into the hand he holds out to be shaken or by an air of brooding suspicion. The prospective purchaser, eyeing him with disbelief as if he were a saucer of half-crowns in a cloakroom, whips out a bradawl and vanishes into the counter breathing harshly.

Given due warning that the mistake has been made our man heads for his boat intent upon whipping out as much gear as he can before customers arrive. They find a venerable compass containing a bubble the size of a pickled egg, a heaving line unaccountably bristling with clothes pegs and surprise him in the act of scuttling ashore with the Terylene mainsheet, leaving in its stead a little grey tump of sisal like a helping of school dinner.

The real and unseen sufferers at the sale of a boat are the crews. Suddenly bereft of a billet they are left milling around in distracted circles like earwigs abruptly deprived of their inverted flowerpot. The owner, aware of the dangerous knowledge they share, touching on mummied-up exhaust pipe and gaffboards which munch away like a sink waste disposal unit, welcomes their presence during his sales talk the way a cracker manufacturer welcomes a Consumer Research team.

Old Harry, who can sell a boat and for an additional fiver chuck in the green buoy which marks its position as a mooring, takes grave pride in the composition of his advertisements—little literary gems hinting at heart-rending self-denial.

'Must sacrifice for quick sale', he sobs, 'converted racing scallop-drudger, racing record, racing engine, maintained regardless cost, recent survey, £350 o.n.o.' This little effusion brings in a rush of bicycle-clipped enquirers in spectacles and berets, all intent upon knocking off the odd fifty and making sail at once for Georgetown.

'A real little beauty', Old Harry enthuses for the benefit of a sceptical audience. He slaps a fond hand on the fantail and immediately two portholes fly open amidships and the cable goes roaring out of the hawse.

Met. Trickery

OLD HARRY REGARDS the 'met trick' system as some kind of conjuring act in poor taste to be examined with the cautious contempt of a diner exploring some foreign dish preparatory to sending it back. Convinced that the Decimal Place is a cul-de-sac in Soho he remains faithful to inch, foot and fathom and he prowls the chandlery measuring accurately with knuckle, seaboot and outflung arms (exit two wealthy yachtsmen in two-tone shoes with concertina-d cigars clamped between their teeth).

Sales assistants are bitterly aware that Old Harry, when measuring rope, has an armspan of unstinted generosity. Keeping their distance warily like dogs round a hedgehog, they wait until his arms have finished flailing, then they double his fathoms, call them metres, add **VAT**, date and dialling code to the price and give him a free tide-table.

No caravan camper, struggling to unship his dentures in the communal washroom ('Tell Franfiff I've juft finiffed'), juggles with such shifty dexterity as your decimal-minded Briton with his ready reckoner. Enunciating with the smacking relish of a calf at a salt-lick, he reels off kms, gms, mms and lits with new-found fluency, and phones YACHTING MONTHLY editorial with queries about the weight of his kedge—in kilos. A long silence and heavy breathing greets him.

The rest of us, forlornly standing around clutching our useless foot rulers, are properly lumbered. 'Actually,' we say, in our best Empire Building voices, 'a metre is really only a yard-and-a-bit and two of them make a-bit-over-a-fathom.' It will be a long time before the leadsman's cry of 'By the mark nine point one four metres' stirs the souls of listeners ashore, but not so long before Godfrey, working up steam for his Yachtmaster Coastal and with his little ready reckoner in his hand, makes *his* mark. 'Just remember your decimal point and you'll be bang on every time,' he predicts, moments before his 1·219 keel slams into a 0·914 mudbank. This is the moment when cousin Percy pops his head up from down below to announce, '10cm in the pumpwell skipper'. A fist hammers him into the deck like a peg in an educational toy.

The wife who asks her husband to powder her shoulders *after* he has donned his dinner jacket and dead bat tie wins a blast of disapproval only

Old Harry's Bunkside Book

slightly less than that shown by Old Harry when told the price of a new metric chart. The replacement of his old one, occasioned by a sharp turn to leave a tomato soup stain to port and collision with a spratter revealed that Tanner's Gut, Gashouse Creek and Muckin Reach are all now swept by metric water, a phenomenon responsible for his leaky stern tuck, gribble in his cutwater and a rattle in his clack.

The discovery of Lowest Astronomical Tide level numbed him. That 'they' had pulled the plug on soundings in general was obviously responsible for the usual series of jaw-rattling groundings which punctuate his passages. 'Met Trick water!' he growls, peering over the side at this inferior foreign element, 'Why dog-bite-me there's no *body* in the stuff.'

It is all rather unfair that *we* are having to change. The Continentals (a nomenclature that makes anyone from south of Dover or east of Clacton sound like a trick unicycle act) have it all their own way, dealing with round figures like a metre of this or a kilo of that, while we are stuck with messy near-equivalents. The Erith YC rendition of *Spanish Ladies* on men's supper night is sung with as much enthusiasm as a yachtsman buying rockery stones. 'Oh we had eighty-two-point-thirty-metres and a fine sandy bottom', they chorus dutifully between sips at 568 millilitres of flat ale. Somewhere out at sea, edging his way cm by cm out along a 5·486m bowsprit to muzzle a 7sq m, 311gm jib goes a grim figure. He snags his quintals on the cranze and disappears with a falsetto howl.

The 'environment' (we didn't even know we had one until politicians began bleeping about it) is another mystery to Old Harry, who had always supposed it to be a tract of slagheaps north of Wolverhampton. Pollution, associated with the yellow buoy off the town pier and fat mullet, had never worried him either until he found it referred to statistically in *litres,* whereupon he saw it as a new Met Trick threat.

His own sanitary arrangements on board, innocent of pump and outlet, are confined to a red painted bucket bearing the legend FIRE LCC (an identification rather than an exhortation) and they lack the refinement of your modern 80-use pastel pink and plastic thunder-box. He saw his duty at once. No more for him the wait for the ebb, a shifty look around and look-out-to-loo'rd boys.

Wandering ashore at a marina, bucket in hand, he placed it down on the catwalk and went off to enquire the whereabouts of a Proper Disposal Point. There was a large lady in a skirt that would have fitted a hovercraft, cooking chips aboard her bijou sedan cruiser. Without warning her chip pan caught fire. Raising her fine contralto voice in a call for help she uttered the *dreaded word.*

A little old man with celery ankles and low-slung shorts happened to be passing by. 'Don't worry madam, I used to be a boy scout,' he cried. With this curious and irrelevant piece of information he siezed the bucket and with one swing solved two problems in one.

A Hard Case

HISTORY REVEALS THE 10th century Englishman delivering up his Danegeld with much the same merriment in the rictus of his smile as our present-day yachtsman coughing up his R.Y.A. sub—that is until the legal storm clouds begin to gather. With some Borough Council about to start dumping refuse on the saltings there goes up a howl for justice. No late Sunday traveller hopelessly jerking the handle of a defunct chocolate-raisin machine on a rain-swept Welsh platform, presents a more doleful picture than the yachtsman with his mud berth full of bedsteads.

'They've got a team of trained lawyers' he rejoices, conjuring up a vision of sombre-coated performers juggling with silver dumb-bells.

Not that Borough plans for filling Rankwater Creek needed R.Y.A. intervention. Led by Old Harry, the local mariners pounced upon the first load of junk with touching gratitude, enriching their vessels with pram-wheel and sofa spring and faster than the cursing contractors could unload.

Old Harry, champion of the oppressed, has long been a familiar figure in legal circles. Never missing a chance to appear as witness, he has lost more cases than a work-to-rule baggage clerk and has been handed on from one legal firm to the next like a hot dinner-plate in a canteen.

In his black claw-hammer coat shot with green opalescence like some monster blow-fly looking for the meat-safe (and which he deems appropriate to such dignified occasions) he makes a majestic figure. All heads bow as he enters court but it has yet to be decided whether this is a mark of respect or an exercise aimed at reading the label pinned to the tail of his suit and apparently offering a staggering reduction in the cleaning and dyeing of eiderdowns.

Our tin-and-clapboard sailing clubs fight constantly for survival against protesting residential neighbourhoods.

'Bang, bang, bang morning, noon and night' wail local residents.

'You'll be hearing from our solicitors!' they add, as if announcing some rare choral treat. Then there is the matter of those little huts which stand at a suspicious distance from the club, square, stark and foreboding. Nearby residents weary of watching members scuttle in and out like worker bees bringing home the honey, unite in their common grievance.

'With mother in the front room it's not very nice is it~' they mutter '... and you can see the tops of their heads...!'

Old Harry's summer cruise, routed to take in rusted-up swing bridges and sailors' walks, brings in its wake a feast of legal activity. Many a bridge-keeper, with lower lip reaching quiveringly for his soup spoon is blasted into historic activity by Harry's fog horn while waterfront residents, athwart his righteously-trodden path, reach for pen and paper after he has gone by.

'It was not...' they write, 'so much that he balanced along my haha as the fact that when he fell, he flattened my little pixie.'

The military, too, come under his frowning attentions. His topsail, a familiar shape in the sights on coastal gunnery ranges, progresses along the horizon at a rate which would make the growth of a stalactite seem fast.

'Bushy-topped vessel at six thousand,' intone subalterns all cleft chin and sheepskin, 'Just the once sir....'

On the occasions when Old Harry appears in court on his own behalf his counsel outlines a picture of a broken old man which reduces the room to a stricken silence broken only the odd stifled sob. Once in the box though and the trumpeting peroration blasts off wigs like baby owls homing to a ruined steeple.

His advisers, having stomached the case of the sack in the supermarket and argued with flagging spirits over the matter of the ornamental anchor chain (litter bins at ten fathom intervals) have finally refused to accept his custom.

'We regret that we cannot handle your briefs', they wrote fastidiously.

Touched by this unexpected bashfulness and making an appropriate selection from his wardrobe Old Harry made the presentation in person.

'Keep em',' he said, raising a hand to stem the babble of gratitude 'all they need is a new bit 'o codline'.

A Flare for Invention

A YACHTSMAN AND his distress signals is like the seasoned and cautious traveller who won't stir without a toilet roll in his luggage. Without them neither feels safe, both hope never to need them and both know that there is no acceptable substitute for either in case of emergency.

There is the owner who buys the cheapest possible pack (of flares), or is motivated more by an artistic appreciation of colour ('he gets it from his mother's side you know') than by stern judgement. The yachtsman regards his flares with begrudgement, like a commuter with his costly season ticket—having paid more than he can afford for something he didn't want in the first place.

In any case all too many yachtsmen start popping off long before their own resourcefulness is exhausted, and for reasons that vary from an inability to receive Radio One to a desire for company. Genuine cases tend to delay too long or to divine, with an uncanny accuracy, the moment when lifeboatmen ashore are about to put on their carpet slippers. Regarding the RNLI as an adjunct to the National Health Service, they summon the life-boat with the same easy confidence applied to their local GP ('My mother's got this nasty looking knee, doctor'). Both invitations are attended with promptness unrelieved by deep interest or pleasure.

'I see sir,' says the cox of the ILB, wringing water out of his beard, So you really must be back in Town by 10.30. Oh naturally you sent up six parachute flares and a Day Smoke sir. You could also have exhibited Flames In The Vessel sir, . . . an internationally accepted distress signal of great efficacy sir.' The owner, unaware of this method, shows immediate interest. The Coxswain smiles evilly. 'Now here's the way to go about it sir . . .,' he explains.

Old Harry would never admit to being in need of RNLI assistance, although on the occasion of being reported to be perilously aground on a pinnacle he received the arrival of the life-boat with good grace. 'What's this then? Flag Day?' he asked humorously, 'Since you lot just happen to be passing by I might accept a bit of a pluck off.' The crew in their boat, like an Easter nest of stubbly yellow chicks, wrapped him in a blanket and dragged him struggling into their cuddy where they plied him with very

Old Harry's Bunkside Book

hot water bottles and practised the Schafer Method on him with unnecessary energy and grim satisfaction.

Old Harry's flares were time-expired when Grace Darling was still being potted. Great dun-coloured cylinders with conical wooden warheads and a 6ft pole, they are guaranteed to be armour piercing on the way down, in the unlikely event that they should ever go up. In fact, as he managed to demonstrate while using a blowlamp to discourage some fungus in his futtocks, they went sideways.

At the time, he was laid alongside the Town Quay, and like some awesome godly vengeance from Norse mythology, it went screaming up the High Street. A lady traffic warden, bending to read a meter, straightened up with a twang of elastic and dropped a couple of digits, while a solicitor's clerk, up to no good in firm's time, slammed the desk drawer and flattened his Dinky Toys. A cop on point duty was left pirouetting heavily and bounding around like Dr Scholl testing out a new corn plaster, but it was a gossiping matron, shaped like a middle ground buoy and taking leave of her friend, who rounded the show off. 'My goodness, I'm all behind today?' she said with unwitting candour, 'Bye, I'm going to fly now!'

Old Harry is reported to the Coastguard with the regularity of suburban nature lovers hailing the first cuckoo. Old ladies in seafront bed-sitters, maintaining their 24-hour vigil over the shameful goings-on in the wildly rocking beach huts, also follow his erratic maritime manoeuvres with puzzled attentiveness. 'No madam,' says a sighing policeman to his telephone, 'What you can see is probably a trick of the light or a large telescope at a low angle.' 'No madam,' says a weary Coastguard, 'what you can see is probably a yachtsman rucking his nock.' 'Yes madam,' says a yawning RNLI Secretary at 4 am, elbow on pillow, 'We're always delighted to be told when you think you've seen something funny off the end of the pier. Perhaps you'll give me more details about this side-splitting occurrence.'

Ever a scientist at heart and with an eye to improvement, Old Harry once set about manufacturing rockets capable of greater duration and altitude. Using an ancient Chinese formula, handed down (with alacrity) until it reached Barking Municipal Free Library, he compounded sulphur, burnt straw and saltpetre with a variety of unguents and inflammable nostrums, packing all into a jumbo size Squezy bottle and attaching thereto a stout curtain pole. Realising the need to try out his prototype far from the sea, he got out his bike and headed for open country. and haunts of coot and tern − both, at that time, blissfully unaware of what was coming their way.

An ardent bicyclist in his youth, his plunging knickerbockered legs had shied more horses than Stephenson's Rocket. His career in the Barking Creek Wheelers Club came to an abrupt end when he caught his wheels in the tramlines. The open doors of the Depot received his hurtling form like Valhalla opening to Eric the Red, but it was the buttocks of a hulking inspector, bowed low as he sank his grizzled muzzle into a pint ot tea, that ended both his careering and his career.

Old Harry's Bunkside Book

Strapping the huge pyrotechnic to the crossbar of his study machine, he headed for the countryside, pedalling firmly and at a pace just adequate to preserve equilibrium. Mentally congratulating the Authorities on their wisdom in providing a white line along which he could navigate and acknowledging the friendly cries of passing motorists, he made good time up the motorway. It was both unfortunate and coincidental that the red hot dottle from his pipe should have ignited his blue touch paper. There was a roar and a great gout of flame from beneath his tool bag. Within seconds his speed attained and exceeded the prohibited 70-mile limit.

With admirable presence of mind he raised his feet to the handlebars in the stylish mode of his youth and began overtaking vehicles at a rate that left them swerving wildly in his wake. A nun in a Morris 1000, forsaking her wheel and fumbling for her beads, made a surprise and unauthorised entry at the front door of a Little Chef; a Dutch driver of a juggernaut was left juggling with his Bols. The police car that took up pursuit stood no chance at all. Losing his way in the smoke cloud, its driver took a slip road in error and arrested a bicycling midwife.

With one final resounding explosion and an eruption of stars, Prince of Wales Feathers, cinders, spanners and smouldering melton trouser seat, the display came to an end and Old Harry, decelerating, slid to a halt under the baleful eye of a motorbike cop, with rockinghorse teeth and an open notebook. 'I should never have eaten them sprouts,' commented Old Harry.